SHAME
AND BODY IMAGE

Culture And
The Compulsive Eater

Barbara McFarland, Ed.D.
Tyeis L. Baker-Baumann, M.S.

Health Communications, Inc.
Deerfield Beach, Florida

Barbara McFarland, Ed.D.
Tyeis L. Baker-Baumann, M.S.
Eating Disorders Recovery Center
Cincinnati, Ohio

Library of Congress Cataloging-in-Publication Data

McFarland, Barbara
    Shame And Body Image: Culture and the compulsive eater/
Barbara McFarland, Tyeis L. Baker-Baumann.
        p.   cm.
    Includes bibliographical references.
    ISBN 1-55874-064-3
    1. Eating disorders — Etiology.   2. Shame.   3. Body image.
I. Baker-Baumann, Tyeis L.   II. Title.
    RC552.E18M39   1990   89-28275
    616.85'26071—dc20   CIP

ISBN 1-55874-064-3

Publisher: Health Communications, Inc.
        3201 S.W. 15th Street
        Deerfield Beach, Florida 33442

Dedication

This one is for our grandmothers, Mary Grudzinka Dressel, Julia Iwinski Luczak, Verona Flatter Harless, Juanita Eley Baker and our mothers, Anna Dressel Luczak and Shirley Harless Baker, who deeply influenced the development of our feminine selves.

Acknowledgments

We would like to thank Henry F. Kenkel, M.D., who first taught us about wholeness and helped to center us, personally and professionally. He greatly influenced the philosophy of treatment at the Eating Disorders Recovery Center. Not only did he stimulate us intellectually, but — more importantly — his very presence exuded the power of a unified masculine/feminine self.

Also, we would like to thank Sue McDonald, Clinical Assistant at the Eating Disorders Recovery Center, who facilitated our work and was our Research Assistant, as well.

We would especially like to thank the five patients who were willing to share their shame experiences and art work so that other compulsive eaters could feel less isolated and be better able to externalize their shame and begin their recovery from this devastating addiction. By sharing their experiences, they have also helped counselors and other therapists who treat compulsive eaters to have a better understanding of the compulsive eater's shame experience.

We would like to thank our spouses, Harold and Bill, for their support, patience and understanding during the development of this manuscript.

Contents

Introduction

The *mandala* is an ancient circular symbol of wholeness and harmony, emphasizing the inter-relationship of Heaven, Man and Earth. According to this philosophy, everything in nature is a blend of the *yin* — the female, receptive earth principle — and the *yang* — the male, originating, celestial principle. It emphasizes the wholeness of nature so that an overidentification with either of the two is avoided.

Our Western culture, however, is a one-sided culture in that it favors patriarchal values — productivity, rationality, goal orientation — at the expense of the more interpersonal values traditionally recognized as feminine. This masculine/feminine split and the negation of the feminine principles of life promote shame for both men and women regarding the inner self and the human body. We believe this has been a major contributor to the rise of addictive illnesses in this country but particularly eating disorders.

The female body has become a scapegoat for the culture's shame about its feminine side. This shame has manifested itself in the American woman's obsession with diet, with exercise and even with having surgery so that her body can be an object of pride and measure up to the cultural ideal of beauty and femininity.

Many women are able to withstand these pressures and maintain a more nurturing and realistic relationship with their bodies. However, there are women, especially those from dysfunctional families, who have a disturbed body image as well as a disturbed relationship with food. An early family history of shaming makes a woman more vulnerable to the cultural dictate of feminine beauty and acceptability as a measure of value and self-worth. These are the women who are prone to develop an addictive relationship with food in order to hide the deeper wounds of their personal shame.

In our work with hundreds of eating disorder patients, we have recognized a universal shame theme that permeates the core of both their emotional lives and their physical selves. It is a deep and abiding shame of the feminine aspects of the self.

Compulsive eaters experience a dual shame bind: the shame of the inner self and the shame of the body. The feminine spirit, which is viewed by our culture as weak, passive, dependent and emotional, and the female body, which has become an object of idealization, comprise the dual shame bind for compulsive eaters.

The shame themes that emerge from this devaluing of the feminine are particularly centered around independence and control. Our patients constantly struggle with feelings of shame because they need relationships and because they have feelings; they have viewed their needs and feelings as weak and shameful. They desperately want to be independent and self-sufficient, rational and in control, in charge of their feelings, needs and appetites.

They have equated dieting and thinness with the cultural stereotypical masculine qualities of power and independence; they equate binging and fat with the cultural stereotypical feminine qualities of weakness and dependence.

They live out our cultural, collective shame/pride dichotomy, which views the masculine value system of power, competitiveness, independence, self-sufficiency and rationality as good — therefore qualities to be proud of — while emotions, need for others and harmony, traditionally viewed as feminine qualities, are viewed as inferior and therefore shameful. The idealization of the masculine aspects has created a loathing for feminine qualities, which creates sparks of shame in the individual every time she experiences a more feminine urge.

People with eating disorders act out the cultural schizo-phrenia regarding our masculine and feminine sides. One is seen as good and worthy of pride, while the other is viewed as bad and shameful.

There is a great, deep sense of shame in needing others, in valuing relationships. This need is viewed as an imma-turity, a co-dependency, an addiction in itself. That is the shame our patients speak about most.

The body has become the object which tells the world whether or not a person is strong enough, controlled enough, powerful enough. The body, as an object of shame, becomes a mask for no matter how thin or fit the body is, it can never eradicate the deeper shame within. But it has become a wonderful distraction, an effective way to create a culturally acceptable image which says to the world, *Look at me. I am good enough.* Since the inner shame cannot be diminished by an image, it continues to be a part of our emotional lives. It fuels our need to continue making the image more and more perfect, with the desperate hope that once it is good enough, the inner shame will finally quiet itself.

Many of our patients experience a secondary advantage from their obesity. As long as they stay overweight, they can avoid facing their inner shame. They stay fixated on the belief that weight loss will make them happy and acceptable to others, that it will make them much less needy and much more in control and independent. By shedding pounds, they believe they can shed their feminine side.

Often, the words "feminist" or "feminine side" provoke negative images and feelings in us. We like to believe that things have changed since the 1960s and that women have made great strides in achieving equal status with men.

We do not intend here to discuss the status of women's economic or social equality. What we are committed to discussing is the basic belief that all human beings, regardless of gender, have both a masculine and a feminine side. Each side has its own unique strengths which, when juxtaposed, becomes a complete and resilient whole. Many individuals in our culture today experience a sense of inner emptiness, a hole that causes feelings of restlessness, uncertainty and fragmentation. It is through the appreciation and valuing of both the masculine and feminine aspects of being human that we come to close up the gap within. The emptiness will no longer exist. Once we can respect and value the differences of both sides of ourselves, seeing each as offering unique gifts, we are better able to function in our relationship with ourselves and with one another. Being divided against ourselves (overvaluing the masculine qualities and negating the feminine urgings) forces us to continue searching frantically for what's missing. That search is what compulsive eating, chemical dependency, workaholism, etc. are all about. These are all unsuccessful efforts to fill up the emptiness.

Ultimately this is achieved through a meaningful relationship with a Higher Power. Although this book is not about spirituality, we do believe that in order for an individual to develop a positive spiritual relationship with a Higher Power he or she must first be able to embrace both the masculine and feminine aspects of the self. The formation of a spiritual relationship is a process that is contingent upon an internal wholeness which comes with accepting and appreciating the masculine and feminine sides. This book focuses on the initial steps necessary to heal the spiritual emptiness created by unhealthy shame.

First, we explore the meaning of shame, the differences between shame and guilt and between shame and pride. This then serves as a basis for understanding the shame experience.

Next, we summarize the most recent explanations and theories regarding the shame experience. Because we believe shame formation is rooted in the early relationship between primary caregiver and infant, we focus on and summarize Gershen Kaufman's theory of shame. We discuss our differences regarding separation/individuation as a universal developmental stage and we examine how this has fostered shame in all of us.

We examine the culture's role in shame formation as well as the history of the female body as the object of shaming, through the culture's idealization of masculinity.

We explore the factors that influence body image development, including cultural, parental and peer expectations and physical elements such as aging and deformity.

We describe five case histories which exemplify the shame themes of compulsive eaters.

Finally, we discuss recovery strategies for the body and for the feminine side.

1

Understanding Shame

Shame. Think of a time in your life when you felt deeply ashamed. Stop for a few moments, close your eyes and re-enact the shameful or embarrassing moment in your mind's eye. As you replay the scene, what do you feel? A churning in your stomach? A flushed face? A shiver down your spine? Perhaps the memory is so painful that you have a strong need to turn away from the image in your head.

Shame is a powerfully painful and complex feeling state. It has its own neural pathway to the autonomic nervous system and more often than not produces blushing and increased heart rate. Consequently, the shame experience involves a greater awareness of the body, unlike other affective states.

It is only in the last few years that shame, as an affective state, has been given attention in the clinical literature.

There is a growing interest among professionals in the emotion of shame, particularly in the addictive illness arena. Practitioners are beginning to recognize that feelings of shame need more attention in the therapeutic relationship.

The nature of shame in itself is the reason why its centrality to addictive illness, perhaps all illness, has been minimized. Due to the emotional pain it invokes, we want to avoid it. Because of what this shame may be telling us about ourselves, it is very difficult to communicate about it.

In addition to the personal dilemma that shame creates, we believe it has long gone unrecognized, misdiagnosed and mistreated because we are a shame-based culture. Because of our society's overemphasis on competition, we are more motivated to hide our shame and to see the shaming process as normal. (We will discuss the definition and ramifications of a shame-based culture later.)

Historically, shame has been seen as a symptom, a response to a personality disorder or moral weakness. For example, the alcoholic should feel ashamed because his drinking behaviors are proof of his lack of moral development.

As our knowledge and understanding of illness, people and cultures expand, theories and perceptions about the shame experience need to be reevaluated. Shame is now being defined not solely as a by-product of addiction or psychiatric problems but as a contributor to their development. Shame has come to be seen as less symptomatic, more causal.

There are many facets to the shame experience, nuances of uncomfortable feelings that tug and pull at one's very soul. Although we have all experienced shame, it is very difficult to assign words to the actual feelings because language is inadequate to communicate so complex a human experience. Although universal, shame is unique in that there is variability among individuals; what is felt as abject shame by one person may be mildly embarrassing to another. This fact helps us to more fully understand the impact of family, peer group and the culture in general on the development of shame in each individual.

The range of the shame experience includes embarrassment, humiliation, disgrace, dishonor and self-consciousness.

The origins of the word "shame" are obscure but scholars believe it is derived from an Indo-European root *(s)kem*, or *(s)kam* which means to cover oneself. When we experience shame, we generally cannot maintain eye contact and we typically avert our gaze, having a strong desire to physically pull away, to shrink back and disappear. We literally want to become invisible or sink into the ground.

Marissa, one of our patients who was a compulsive eater and morbidly obese, recalled her most shameful experience when she was eight years old. "I was with a group of children at lunchtime when we decided to play a game that required two teams. I was standing next to my friend when one of the older kids started shouting, 'Hey, fatso! You could be on a team all by yourself!' The whole group started laughing and moved away from me. There I stood all alone with what seemed like a hundred fingers pointing at me. I suddenly felt a deep, hot flush come over my face and I desperately wanted to be swallowed up by the ground on which I stood."

Exposure And Defectiveness

There are two common factors in the inner experience of shame: exposure and defectiveness. Once again, return to your shameful image and answer these questions: In what way did you feel exposed? What part of your self was exposed? In what way did you feel defective as a result of this experience?

Shame generally follows a moment of exposure. It is as though something we were concealing from the world is suddenly at center stage in public view. This exposure heightens our self-awareness to a painful degree in which our entire consciousness is flooded with an awkward sense of ourselves. This heightened self-awareness is coupled with intense feelings of being inferior, defective, not good enough, fundamentally bad as a person.

In her treatment group, Marissa shared that it wasn't until the incident described that she realized that being fat was *bad*; that, in fact, there was something *wrong* with her. She said that since that time, she has never felt the same about herself. To this day, being in a group promotes strong feelings of self-consciousness for her. She continues to fear any further exposure.

The Bipolarity Of The Shame Experience

Experiences of shame expose our most sensitive, vulnerable dimensions.

Leon Wurmser, in his book, *The Mask of Shame* (1), views the shame experience as bipolar. The object pole is the person *in front of whom* we are ashamed while the subject pole is that aspect of ourselves *of which we feel ashamed*. Using Marissa as an example, being ridiculed for her size by her peers is the shame felt in front of others (object pole); she also felt shame for being different, that is, fat (subject pole). Until then, she had not yet developed any association of her weight with lack of control or self-discipline.

Wurmser gives the example of the child who wets the bed. (1) Feelings of shame include being discovered by the mother and having to deal with her disapproval and scolding (the object pole). However, the child is also ashamed of wetting the bed because it is an indication of a loss of control (the subject pole).

The experience of shame can either be an exposure in front of another individual or group or seen as a result of having failed oneself. Regardless, shame promotes intense feelings of powerlessness and impotence and gives us a concept of ourselves as dependent, inadequate and inept. Since the defect is inherent in our personhood, there is no way to make it better or fix it. It is original sin, with no baptism or forgiveness at hand.

Due to the complexity of the shame experience for compulsive eaters, involving a reciprocal interchange between bodyshame and selfshame (concepts we will discuss in greater detail), their shame vacillates between being ashamed of their bodies which can be seen by the world (object pole) and what their fatness represents (lack of control/weakness) and says about their inner self (subject pole). In our work with compulsive eaters, patients enter treatment with an overwhelming sense of shame over their loss of control over food and the size, shape and weight of their body. But as treatment progresses, attention to shame shifts from food, body and weight to other life experiences which devalued their sense of self long before food, weight or body became an issue.

In her treatment group, Marissa shared, "I can remember that as a teenager I felt twinges of shame whenever I saw a thin, shapely girl's body on television, in magazine ads, at school, at football games, everywhere I went. I remember hating myself when I looked at my body in the mirror. Now that I look back, I think I eventually just became numb to the shame I felt about my body. It didn't go away, it just went underground. I wouldn't let myself think I was so fat. But whenever my denial was shattered, whether by a critical comment from my mother or when I saw a picture of myself, the shame feelings resurfaced in a violent, intense surge of emotion."

Well into the program Marissa gradually began to share her deep feelings of inadequacy about forming and maintaining relationships. Her treatment themes shifted from her preoccupation with bodyshame to a focus on her inner self. "I realize now that even as a preschool child, I felt I was different. I always thought it started with that incident in the playground but now I am aware that I felt self-conscious at home with my family, even before I started school." This became obvious to Marissa when she brought early childhood photos to our treatment group which clearly revealed that she was not particularly overweight as a young child. In several photos, however, her facial expression reflected fear and sadness.

Shame Coverups

If we have enough shame-based interactions and experiences, we are likely to develop a shame-based identity. An individual has a shame-based identity when her way of looking at herself (emotionally, physically and spiritually) centers on the internalized belief that she is bad or innately inferior: *There is something wrong with me. If anyone finds out, I will be lost and abandoned. Everyone will hate me —* that is the theme of her life. This powerful sense of vulnerability is emotionally intolerable, so certain defense mechanisms are developed to protect the individual from further emotional harm.

It is important to understand that all of us have emotional defense mechanisms. These developed early in our lives to protect us from being overwhelmed by the world around us. Defense mechanisms are necessary building blocks to the development later of a sense of self. When these defense mechanisms are not steeped in the need to protect us from the unhealthy and degrading experience of shame, they are less rigid and generally used only as a need arises. But if these defense mechanisms are constantly called upon to protect the individual from the pain and persistent fear of shaming, then they will go awry and become a way of life.

Some of the primary ego defenses an individual has to protect herself from overwhelming emotional harm include denial, disassociation, repression, projection, identification, idealization, conversion and depersonalization.

The individual with a shame-based identity will live with her defense mechanisms continuously in place. These defenses will not only determine her roles in interpersonal relationships but will also determine the ways in which she behaviorally and cognitively covers up her shamefulness.

These shame coverups can take many forms. Based on our work with compulsive eaters we have observed that certain coverups are more predominant than others — denial, repression, anger/rage, depression, envy/perfectionism and bodyloathing.

Denial

Denial is traditionally viewed as one of the most primitive (and therefore most difficult to change) defense mechanisms. In a positive framework, denial can help people by keeping their worry and concern at a level which will not immobilize them. Not dwelling on all the statistics of traffic fatalities enables us to learn how to drive. Not ruminating about all the things that might happen allows us to travel in airplanes, get married, have babies, learn to swim, etc.

However, denial in response to unhealthy shame results in clouding the individual's ability to perceive facts accurately, to see and remember behaviors and interactions without great distortion. Denial enables self-destructive actions and interactions to continue.

Faith, a bulimic of 14 years, is just now able to understand her own denial. "Until recently, I never saw my binge/purge behavior as a problem. I didn't even identify myself as a bulimic. I told myself that my behavior about food and my obsession with my weight were okay. I'd tell myself that most people behave this way to control their weight — so it wasn't any big deal. After all, we all did it in college . . . My developing dental problems were genetic, not caused by vomiting . . . My mood swings and growing desire to isolate were caused by the way people around me behaved, not because my bulimic behaviors were getting more out of control and unpredictable . . . Now I look back over the past 14 years of my life and wonder what really happened."

Repression

Repression is another primary defense mechanism designed to help each of us experience intolerable feelings with less distress. The numbness and shock that a mother feels when one of her children dies is natural and allows the woman to function for a time, until she can emotionally and cognitively understand what has happened and get the emotional support she needs. But, as with denial, for the shame-based person repression — freezing out or numbing of emotions so completely that we aren't even aware they exist — becomes a way of life.

When Geena, a 42-year-old single woman, came to our treatment center for her initial assessment, she appeared pleasant, bright and articulate. In talking with her about her personal history, Geena related that her father had been alcoholic since she was about ten years old and that her mother had been chronically ill for as long as she could remember. Her older brother, whom she adored and received a great deal of affection from, had abruptly left home to join the service when she was 12. She rarely saw or heard from him thereafter.

During the discussion, Geena was asked several times how she felt about these losses. "I don't know," was her consistent reply. "I've never thought about how I feel." Geena's power of repression was so great she wasn't even aware that it was unnatural for her not to have feelings. For her, a compulsive overweight overeater, food was a sedative that kept her frozen feelings unrecognized and unexpressed.

Anger/Rage

Anger and/or rage, felt consistently, are effective tools for covering up shame. We are not talking here of appropriate anger such as one might feel at being lied to or taken advantage of. Anger and rage as shame coverups are intense emotions that are frequently unpredictable and always out of proportion to the event or situation which has triggered them.

Joe is a very successful businessman, though overweight and chronically unhappy when he entered treatment. One of Joe's main concerns in treatment was his anger. He was known to scream and yell at his employees when common mistakes were made, particularly if a client called to complain. As Joe explored his anger, he realized how inappropriate his behavior actually was. Thinking he had simply not learned to express his anger effectively (both his parents were "screamers"), he immersed himself in the assertiveness literature, committed to practicing assertive behaviors on a daily basis.

Even so, Joe continued to experience intense angry feelings which rationally made no sense to him. Exploring his confusion in group one day, another group member asked Joe to talk more about how he felt when clients called with complaints. Working with the group to identify feelings that his anger might cover up, Joe discovered that he was afraid. He was afraid that when his customers had complaints about his business, their image of him became devalued. He feared they would see him for the fraud he felt himself to be. He felt terribly ashamed of himself but his tirades distracted everyone (including himself) away from the shame.

Depression

Depression is a remarkably complex and frequently misunderstood coverup for shame. By looking at depression as a coverup, we are not suggesting that depression might not have other clinical significance. However, what we discovered among our patients exhibiting symptoms of depression is a combination of repressed emotions, particularly anger, hurt and sadness. These emotions are coupled with a deep sense of shame for not being "a better person."

Clarissa, a 31-year-old bulimic, had been treated for depression on and off since she was an adolescent. She believed for a long time that her depression was either genetic or learned, because her mother had also suffered from depression since Clarissa was about three years old. Her mother had been hospitalized frequently while Clarissa was a young child and during her adolescence. As a result, she was left alone many, many times with her dad and he also was rarely home. As she got older, she was expected to take care of him whenever her mom was in the hospital.

As Clarissa continued in treatment and became involved in grief process work, she recognized the very angry, resentful feelings she had toward both her mother and her father for not being there for her when she was a child. "I hate them both," she said, pounding her clenched fists on the arm of her chair. Almost immediately upon expressing these feelings in group one day, with eyes downcast and her face flushed, Clarissa abruptly stopped talking. After much encouragement from group members to tell what she was feeling, Clarissa blurted out tearfully, "I feel so bad. I'm such a mean and selfish person. How could I be so angry with my parents, especially with my mother who was so sick? They really did the best they could." In time, Clarissa was helped to see that the anger she felt was quite natural. As she became more comfortable with this idea, Clarissa was able to identify her angry feelings more readily. Her depression lifted.

Envy/Perfectionism

In our experience, envy and perfectionism are very intensely developed shame coverups for compulsive eaters. These feelings are initially discussed by patients in relation to their bodies.

The body itself becomes a major source of shame since it does not measure up to the idealized cultural standard of beauty. The fat or imperfect body says to the world, *I am a failure. I am weak, needy and out of control* (bodyshame), and is seen as the signal to the world that what it holds inside is defective and inferior (selfshame). Consequently, the compulsive eater is often consumed with feelings of envy toward other women whose bodies are "perfect," giving out the message, *I am successful, independent and powerful*.

Marissa, in discussing her current lack of social relationships and tendency to isolate, says, "I used to have friends, one really good friend. But, she was extremely pretty and thin and it was just too painful for me to be with her. Whenever we went out together, she got all the attention. I remember one time when a guy began to talk to her at a baseball game. He never once looked at me. It was as though I didn't even exist. Those searing feelings of shame, of not being good enough, pretty enough or thin enough flooded my body, my very soul. Although I didn't realize it at the time, I never called her again and I found excuses not to return her calls. It's just too painful to be around people. I feel much safer being alone . . . with my food."

For compulsive eaters, envy and perfectionism go beyond the body and also include aspects of the self. These themes generally revolve around how they expect themselves to function in relationships. Compulsive eaters have unrealistic standards for themselves and others. This often results in feelings of deep dissatisfaction and disappointment in their relationships.

SueAnn, a 34-year-old bulimic, told the group about a recent interaction she had with her husband. After several weeks in treatment, she became very enthusiastic about all that she had learned regarding her dysfunctional birth family. Since her husband also came from an alcoholic family, she assumed that he would be as excited about her new insights. When she asked him to read a particular book on co-dependency, he exploded and said, "Quit trying to analyze me. My family may have had problems but you're the one who is really screwed up!" SueAnn was devastated. She couldn't understand why her husband didn't want to recover with her. They continued to fight about this well into the evening.

As she shared this, she said, "I don't understand him. He should want to change. He should be happy about the changes I've made. I can't believe he got so angry and told me to leave him alone. I guess he really doesn't love me."

In the course of treatment, SueAnn was able to see that her expectations of her husband and herself were unrealistic. She was better able to accept their differences and recognize that his recovery was not her responsibility. She was able to detach from the belief that his love for her was dependent upon their having the same goals and ideas.

Bodyloathing

As a way of avoiding intimacy and dealing with other painful feelings, many of our patients experience a very deep and abiding bodyloathing. The body becomes a receptacle for intense feelings of rage at being cheated or for being so physically different.

Dana, a 27-year-old compulsive eater, talked constantly at first about how she hated her body. Weekly, she recited a litany of complaints. "I hate my skin. Look at it. It's so putridly white and freckled. I wear long sleeves to hide my fat arms which are totally covered with ugly brown freckles. And look at this nose. It's huge and fat and ugly. And my legs are like tree trunks . . . " Her voice would rise in disgust. "I absolutely despise my body. I just wish I could make it disappear."

It took Dana some time in treatment to realize that much of the anger she felt toward her body was a veiled expression of her inner shame.

The Positive Side Of Shame

Thus far we have focused on the phenomenon of shame at its worst — a culprit in the demise of emotional, spiritual and physical health. However, there is a positive side to the shame experience.

Healthy shame helps us recognize that as human beings we have limits, by allowing us to know and become comfortable with the fact that we are not omnipotent (not-God) (2) and are not expected to be all-knowing, all-capable or perfect.

The positive side of shame not only allows us to accept the fact that we make mistakes but also to do what we can to remedy them. It gives us the chance to forgive ourselves and others for being imperfect.

When our shame is not debilitating or "toxic" (3) it serves as an important motivator. (4) It encourages the development of a set of intellectual, physical and social skills that give us a sense of adequacy and competence and allows us to follow and understand group norms. It also motivates us to develop skills and competencies so as to avoid the shame of ineptness within the group.

For example, the child who has never expressed an interest in learning to tie her own shoelaces may suddenly become intent on mastering this task when she enters kindergarten and discovers that almost everyone else knows how. Her desire to be a part of the group and not be embarrassed or set apart motivates her to learn a new skill.

Healthy shame protects our self-integrity by increasing our responsiveness to any indication that our self is being overexposed. For example, when a husband reveals extremely personal information about his wife to strangers in a social setting, the wife, feeling too vulnerable and exposed, will frequently flush with embarrassment and attempt to alter the flow of the conversation.

Shame can also function as a sexual regulator. It is the motivator that leads us to seek privacy for sexual relations. Few people feel comfortable engaging in passionate kissing and sexual touch in public. Shame motivates parents to seek privacy in having their sexual needs met, by choosing appropriate times and places for sexual intercourse. For the most part, adolescents and young adults do the same.

Shame, then, can serve several important functions but primarily, it is a phenomenon that allows us to recognize our human limitations and, conversely, encourages us to keep learning.

Pastoral psychotherapist Carl Schneider (4) views shame as protecting the ongoing process of self-integration. He believes we all need private space, time off from the watchful eyes of others before we go public. This need for rehearsal changes and becomes more complex as we mature. Shame protects this process. What is sheltered is not quite ready for sharing. For example, one of our patients, Mary-Beth, wanted to be able to express her buried feelings of anger toward her mother. But before she could face her mother without embarrassment and awkwardness, she practiced expressing her anger by the use of imagery. When she felt as comfortable as she could get, she was able to start sharing these feelings with her mother. She needed time and space to reduce her feelings of self-consciousness so she could be assertive in this relationship.

Guilt And Shame: What's The Difference?

Guilt and shame are often confused. Shame is more closely related to an inherent sense of the self being flawed or defective. It is linked to one's self-image. Karen Horney proposed a triple concept of the self: the actual self, derived from the sum total of our actual experiences; the real self, a force that lies dormant within us and can be reached if we establish a harmonious wholeness; and the ideal self, which Horney viewed as neurotic and the source of the grandiose aspects of the self. (5) The ideal self is based on feedback from others. The ideal self doesn't always have to be, as Horney says, neurotic, a negative factor in self-image. Actually when viewed in the context of healthy shame, it can be a motivating force to continue striving to reach our potential. Whenever we fall short of our ideal self-image, we may experience shame.

With guilt, we do not use an ideal image as a measure but rather we use ideal actions. Guilt results from actually having done something wrong. The behavior that activates guilt violates a moral or ethical code. Generally, people experience guilt when they have broken a rule or in some way violated their own beliefs or standards. Not accepting or carrying out responsibility can also activate guilt feelings. However, since guilt is associated with behaviors within a broad range of ethics and religion, the activators of guilt vary considerably from individual to individual, from culture to culture and ethnic group to ethnic group.

Guilt is activated in situations where the individual feels personally responsible as a result of his own acts or failure to act. Consequently, with guilt, restitution is possible. With shame, however, there is no restitution. With shame, it's not whether you have *done* anything bad, it's that you *are* bad.

The phenomenology of guilt stimulates a great deal of thought on the part of the person who experiences the guilt. That person not only spends a lot of mental energy preoccupied by the wrongdoing but also conjuring up schemes to make things right. Guilt is often followed by imageries of making amends, facing the person wronged, etc.

Shame, on the other hand, leaves a person speechless; it temporarily befuddles thinking. Shame is too difficult to tolerate so the individual tends to repress or deny the shaming experience. Since restitution is impossible, the individual's sense of self is deeply diminished and the self-image affected.

Another way of examining the differences between guilt and shame is to look at the difference in the meaning of the words "guiltless" and "shameless." Being guiltless is a desired state since it connotes innocence or freedom from blame. Being shameless, on the other hand, refers to a deficit in one's character. To be shameless is considered equal to having no sense of values or morals.

Ernie Kurtz summarizes the difference in his book, *Shame and Guilt: Characteristics of the Dependency Cycle*: "Both guilt and shame involve feeling 'bad' — feeling bad about one's actions (or omissions) in the case of guilt, feeling bad about one's self in shame. Each has to do with the boundaries of the human condition." (6)

Guilt is a response to a transgression while shame occurs when a goal or ideal has not been reached. Wurmser says, "Shame guards the boundary of privacy and intimacy; guilt limits the expansion of power; shame covers up weakness; guilt limits strength. Shame protects an integral image of the self; guilt protects the integrity of an object." (7)

Let's take a look at how guilt and shame can interface. One of our patients, Virginia, is a bulimic in the initial stages of recovery. She recalls that when she was in college, as her binging went more and more out of control, she would steal food. She stole food on a fairly regular basis during her senior year from her roommates and from the local grocery store where one of her roommates worked. She was never caught but her roommates developed a standard joke about the Midnight Stalker who crept into their dorm at night and devoured their food. In response to their ongoing frustrations, everyone eventually began locking up and hiding their food.

Even though it's been six years since she graduated from college, whenever she sees her old roommates, Virginia feels a deep sense of shame about herself. She avoids contact with them. One day she actually hid behind some clothes racks when she saw one of them shopping in a local department store. Her shame centers around her feeling of defectiveness because of her bizarre relationship with food — which could be exposed by any of her roommates. She also reports feeling terribly guilty over stealing food since she sees herself as a very honest and ethical person and has never stolen anything else in her life. She feels as though she behaved in a way that was inconsistent with her ideal self-image. She looks at her eating disorder as a very shameful part of herself that must be kept well hidden.

Virginia indicated that whenever anyone comments positively that she can be trusted, she remembers how she stole food and she cannot allow herself to feel good about the praise.

Shame And Pride:
Two Sides Of The Same Coin

Pride is one of the seven deadly sins — deadly in that sinful pride is equated with arrogance and satisfaction in having power and superiority over others. It fosters grandiose feelings of being *better than*.

Arrogant pride is called *hubris* in Greek. However, there is a healthy pride which the Greeks refer to as *philotimo* (8), meaning self-respect. Pride, coupled with humility, fosters a feeling of joy in being human, an acceptance of the self.

Shame and pride are inextricably linked with one's self-image. As we have discussed, shame is a feeling that makes us more self-conscious. Pride is an affective state that also makes us more self-conscious but in a positive way. Shame is a sign of negative attention to the self while pride is a sign of positive attention to the self. Too much unhealthy shame and too much arrogant pride are dangerous and destructive.

Pride involves a desire to share what one is feeling proud of whereas shame promotes a desire to conceal or hide. Donald Nathanson (9) believes that pride and shame are an oscillation between the public and the private. Pride, a happy emotion, makes us want to share with others, to display, to broadcast. Shame, a painful emotion associated with privacy, secrecy and modesty, promotes uncomfortable feelings.

According to Nathanson (9), in early development, pride is often associated with joy. A toddler experimenting with the range of her vocal chords, shrieks wildly and her face is filled with joy and triumph in her ability to produce such powerful sounds. Parents and relatives smile with approval in spite of the piercing noise which accompanies the accomplishment. However, in adulthood, pride is viewed with distrust. It is frequently linked with conceit, weakness and, according to Nathanson (9), is linked dangerously close to the affect of shame, which is supposed to be its opposite. He goes on to say that the adult is much more sensitive to being exposed, as any self-disclosure carries with it the risk of being shamed. "Adult pride cleaves somewhat from joy and links ambivalently to shame." (10)

Children who grow up in functional families have a much easier time boasting about their achievements. They can risk showing the need to be openly admired and valued. Children from shame-based families have a much more difficult time. Research (9) indicates that all adults have difficulty expressing pride in their achievements due to the fear of rejection and overexposure. A history of interpersonal rejections often forces the adult to shrink away from being openly loved, admired or valued. According to Nathanson (9), because pride contains healthy self-love and the assurance of being loved by others, it can also inspire envy and jealousy; therefore it can potentially precipitate an attack or a criticism from others. Consequently, the expression of adult pride is very carefully guarded and particularly so for shame-based adults.

Pride And Comparison

Nathanson describes a relationship between the shame/pride axis and the mechanism of comparison. (9) During our early development, we, as children, were always being compared — compared to mother — "You have your mother's eyes" — to father — "You sure got your dad's temper" — and to other relatives. In addition to that, we live in a culture where everything about us is measured — our height, weight, intelligence, etc. Children are not only compared to each other but also to siblings, cousins, neighbors and media stars — "Why can't you be as smart and ambitious as your cousin?"

This tendency to compare, according to Nathanson (9), is what promotes feelings of shame or pride in the individual, depending on who he is being compared to and how he is being compared.

In dysfunctional families who are daily experiencing unrecognized yet pervasive unhealthy shame, members compare themselves and each other in a negative or manipulating manner. To see each family member as an individual with his own thoughts, feelings, needs and desires is too threatening. Such a process would promote intimacy and, because of the sense of vulnerability this fosters, it is the shame-based person's greatest fear.

Dysfunctional families, therefore, develop roles, rules and coverups designed to keep individual members from being too exposed to each other. The collective *we* of the family keeps them, as individuals, from being too exposed to the world.

The forms of comparison that dysfunctional families use to cover up shame vary from the subtle to the obvious. For example, the son constantly told by his irate

mother that he is just like his alcoholic dad is being bla-
tantly compared and accosted by his mother's shame at
being married to an alcoholic. However, many forms of
shame-based comparisons and manipulations are out-
wardly more subtle, yet just as potent.

Jesse, at 36, was a hard-driving professional saleswo-
man who was extremely upset by her compulsive eating
behaviors and her general dissatisfaction with life. Jesse
grew up in a large family, relatively isolated in a rural
farming community. She talked with great pride about
her maternal grandmother who came to this country
from Ireland when she was only nine. Grandmother was
orphaned soon thereafter and was seen by the family as
the person who carried them through the Great Depression. "She was so strong and together. She was
always working. I don't think I ever saw her cry or get
down about anything. She always said, 'Never let anything get you down.' 'Bite the bullet!' was her favorite
retort whenever someone in the family talked about
problems they were having."

By virtue of the family's idealization of her grandmother, Jesse was taught always to be strong, always to
be busy and she was shamed into never having any feelings that might interfere with being productive (or call
into question the family's belief that to be strong was to
be good).

What Jesse didn't know until much later was that her
grandmother was often ridiculed as a child and later as an
adult for her Irish accent and ethnic customs. In her neighborhood, she was frequently shamed for being different.
Her grandmother's shame coverup was to work hard; proving to everyone that she was indeed good enough.

To conceal their shame, many dysfunctional families
focus on the right image which centers on body, weight
and appearance, especially for its female members.

Faye, a 22-year-old bulimic, was the daughter of two
adult children of alcoholics. Her maternal grandmother
had been a compulsive overeater who became morbidly
obese. Faye's parents were very fitness-oriented and con-

stantly encouraged and coaxed their children to participate in all kinds of sports. Faye was led into competitive gymnastics and did fairly well but when she began to fill out at puberty, she reported that her mother "freaked out." Faye's mother, who had been so embarrassed and humiliated by her own mother's obesity, was not about to have a fat daughter. Faye was put on a strict diet and exercise regimen and was constantly watched by her mother for any stray pounds. At the age of 11, Faye couldn't see that her mother's reaction was the result of her shame over her own mother. Faye believed her mother was deeply and only ashamed of her. Fearing alienation from her mother, Faye stuck to the regimen and even found creative ways to get around it (purging) when the temptation to eat pizza with her friends was just too strong.

Often, innocently enough, parents use comparisons to vent their frustrations or in an attempt to motivate their children to succeed or to behave in a certain manner. "Why can't you win scholarships like your cousin Joey?" or "Well, your sister's the good looking one but at least you have some artistic abilities." Sentiments like these are frequently expressed by shame-wounded parents who then wound their own children with shaming messages.

Pride And Competition

Pride shifts from being a positive affect to a more ambivalent emotion when comparison moves into the arena of competition. Competitiveness promotes one-upmanship. There has to be a winner and there has to be a loser. Pride results from winning whereas defeat results in humiliation.

Nathanson (9) believes that any time we try to rate ourselves, we invoke the shame/pride axis. Winning at something or achieving gives us a sense of pride, whereas failing intensifies the shame feeling. Competition keeps us evaluating ourselves or some quality of ourselves against those of someone else. That someone else can be a collective ideal such as certain body types or multiple role expectations, for example, breadwinner, supermom, seductress. Women expect and are expected by others to adhere to this ideal in order to be viewed as competent and successful — therefore lovable. Compulsive eaters stay forever stuck in comparisons, with their bodies as whipping posts.

For compulsive eaters, there is a constant shifting from pride to shame, which manifests itself in dieting and overeating behaviors. Patients report a tremendous sense of pride in being able to diet and this increases with weight loss. Their pride comes from the belief that they have regained control. Being able to diet and lose weight is seen as proof for themselves and everyone else that they are not weak-willed or lazy.

When compulsive eaters diet, they are not only striving to control what they eat and to lose pounds but they are also striving to attain the culture's ideal body type. The belief in the ideal is, *Once I'm thin, everything will be all right. When I'm thin, all my bad feelings about myself will disappear. I'll be on top of things. I'll be in control.*

This idealization of control is an effort, albeit unconscious, to keep compulsive eaters from facing the reality of their eating disorder and the shame they secretly experience but are too fearful to talk about and face. This pride, often referred to as "false" pride, is built on a precarious foundation of shame. During the initial phase of the dieting ritual, compulsive eaters experience an *emotional high* with their new found control. It is potent enough to overshadow the underlying sense of shame and the persistent unconscious knowledge that the control is false and limited. As the dieting high diminishes with time and compulsive eaters are confronted with uncomfortable feelings and cravings to eat forbidden foods, their security in dieting quickly dissipates.

As soon as the individual goes off the diet, she swings into a deep sense of shame. Deviations from the diet may range from a single bite of forbidden food to an all-out binge. But the shame returns in full force the moment the compulsive eater recognizes that despite all her efforts, her control has failed to be good enough.

Frequently, in the initial phases of treatment, patients will verbalize a cognitive understanding of the disease of compulsive overeating. But secretly they harbor a belief that somehow they will be different and ultimately be able to control their eating disorder. Often these patients are very successful in changing their compulsive eating behaviors and they develop much pride in their ability to stop binging and/or purging. However, early in recovery the pride remains precarious due to its close association with shame. Patients may be steeped in shame, unpredictably at times, because they consciously or unconsciously continue to compare themselves with and compete with others. A good case in point is Lauren.

An overweight 30-year-old compulsive eater, Lauren desperately wanted to stop her binge behaviors. After entering our program, her binging diminished dramatically and consequently she began to lose weight. Lauren felt particularly proud of her ability not only to reduce her binging but also to lose some weight. In group, she indicated that she was going to visit her sister, whom she had not seen in a few months. Lauren kept her compulsive eating a secret from everyone in her family so her sister was unaware of her participation in treatment. Lauren told the group she was so excited about seeing her sister so she could flaunt her slimmer figure. When the others in the group talked with her about how dangerous this kind of thinking was, she brushed them off with a gesture — "Don't worry. I know this is an addiction and there is more to it than simple weight loss!"

Well, when she returned to the group session after the visit to her sister, she was late. She actually slunk into the room, slumped, eyes downcast, arms folded tightly across her chest. When we asked her how the visit went she said, "Just fine." As the group pressed her for more information, she became angrier and angrier. "I didn't come here to be interrogated," she said in a hostile voice soon followed by tears. Group members encouraged Lauren to share what had happened since she was reacting this way to their simple questions.

It seems that when Lauren arrived at her sister's house, her sister blurted out that she had been going to a local diet club and had lost 25 pounds. As Lauren looked at her sister, she reported feeling intense feelings of envy because she had not lost as much weight. The envy was transformed into deep feelings of inadequacy and shame. What she had felt so proud of the day before became a deep source of shame. By comparing herself to her sister, Lauren felt inadequate, a failure. She went home that night and binged.

Each competitive situation ends either in being *better than* or *not good enough*. In Lauren's case her pride was easily shattered and replaced by shame because her weight loss was not good enough compared to her sister's. Even if the individual "wins" there is still the fear that the win is not good enough, so the pride must be hidden or minimized to prevent shame taking its place. After Lauren began to process and externalize her feelings of shame, she renewed her commitment to her recovery. However, from that point on she found it very difficult to express any genuine pride in her abstinence.

If an individual feels a deep sense of shame about some attribute or about the self as a whole, this interferes with the ability to allow any healthy pride or joy. It is too risky to boast since the attention it calls might result in ridicule or rejection, leaving the individual open to the pain of shame.

Gender Myths And Shame

Our hierarchical culture also places a high value on the stereotypically masculine qualities of competitiveness, individualism, rationality, control, aggression and productivity. These qualities are highly regarded. Stereotypically associated with the feminine are fair play, relationships, emotions and harmony — all generally viewed as weak and inferior.

This cultural system devalues feminine qualities and contributes to feelings of shame in both women and men, who desperately try to deny this vital part of their inner selves. That aspect of their make-up which is emotive, relational, noncompetitive and nurturing is shamed by the cultural ideal of what is good and right (and higher up in the hierarchical system).

Through the centuries, our culture has developed many myths related to gender. These myths are linked to sex role stereotypes. Sex role stereotypes say that an individual is supposed to think a certain way, desire specific things and act a certain way, simply because of being biologically male or female.

Men, according to these gender-linked myths, are supposed to be rational, ambitious, goal-oriented, independent, adventurous leaders. Women, on the other hand, are to be emotional, to love children, to be people-oriented and home-oriented, to be faithful and dependent on the leadership and opinions of the predominant male in their lives.

These gender myths promote shame in that they require both men and women to adhere to specific characteristics which may or may not be accurate for who they really are. They require the overemphasis of certain qualities at the expense of devaluing others.

For example, a man who prefers playing with his children over pursuing the next business deal may be admonished by his co-workers or superiors for not being ambitious enough. If the man is not secure in his sense of what is right for him as a unique individual, he will experience shame and feel diminished in his masculinity. A woman, on the other hand, who is not particularly interested in being a mother but focuses her energy instead on vocational aspirations may be viewed as less feminine and therefore less desirable. Despite her inner urgings, she may limit her ambitions or, at the very least, question her attractiveness as a person and as a female. She may feel shame over her supposed lack of femininity because she does not fit the societal notion of what a female is supposed to be.

Where do these gender myths or sex role stereotypes come from? They come from our culture, which is built on a hierarchical system. Hierarchical systems ascribe certain qualities and traits to individuals, based on such outward characteristics as sex, age, race or religion. Once these have been ascribed, the individuals are given a value within the hierarchical system and placed above or below others accordingly.

In our hierarchical system, for example, Caucasian males are supposedly above (having more value and therefore more power) the men of any other race, all women and all children.

The hierarchical system promotes shame in its members because it separates people from one another and promotes comparisons and competition based on one-upsmanship.

We will talk more about the culture's role in shame formation in a later chapter.

2

Shame, Interpersonal Relationships And The Compulsive Eater

The shame experience has received more and more attention in the clinical literature and among professionals. There are many viewpoints on the shame experience and its role in human development. Some attend to what the individual reports feeling (the actual experience) while others regard shame as a symptom or functional event rather than a direct expression of the feeling experience.

Susan Miller, in her book, *The Shame Experience* (1), does an excellent literature review which we have attempted to summarize.

Psychoanalytic thought (2) regards shame as a functional event and focuses on it as a defense rather than as an expressive event. It says that shame means more than just what it feels like. For psychoanalysts, shame means the opposite of what it feels like. This is generally called reaction formation. The experience is taken to actually be a deception, albeit unconscious, which hides the true motivation.

Freudian theorists (3) view shame as a reaction formation against exhibitionistic impulses. The shame feeling is created to shut out the awareness of the forbidden wishes. This group views shame as the "deputy of sexual morality." The negative self-talk about the self which is the basis of experienced shame is not viewed as actual self-evaluation. Instead it is viewed as a deflector to divert the individual away from the exhibitionistic impulses. For example, a young woman may reprimand herself for her inability to carry on an intelligent conversation with an attractive man as a way to distract herself from her desire to be flirtatious or from any sexual fantasies she may be experiencing.

Another group of writers (4), some who conceptualize shame as functional and others who do not, view shame as resulting from a conflict relating to a specific developmental stage or issue. This group believes shame curtails/ curbs exhibitionistic tendencies regarding a psychosexual stage or feelings about the body rather than the broader "nonsexual or nonphysical aspects of the self." (5) These theorists relate shame to genital inferiority, or to "anal experiences of loss of control or loss of good feelings about body products or to phallic concern with genital size or function." (6) For this group, shame remains inextricably linked to bodily concerns. These theories imply that self-disappointments which generate shame are disappointments in bodily function or appearance. Adult experiences of shame are rooted in childhood shame experiences which focus on the body.

We believe, along with Miller, that it is not enough to assume that a history of shame for an adult is strictly related to earlier experienced shame over body parts or functions. However, body image development, which we shall discuss in a later chapter can be greatly influenced by early parent-child interactions.

Miller (7) points out that those theorists who view shame as a functional event have a very narrow focus since they do not examine or define the core of the shame experience itself. The feeling of shame as one of personal inferiority does not represent a true negative feeling about the self but rather is a way of deflecting attention away from unacceptable impulses.

Viewing shame as a sentinel to impulses, be they sexual or aggressive, does not take into account the expressive function of the shame experience. The shame experience, however painful, can be psychologically meaningful. Helping the individual identify and understand the personal meaning of shame can assist her in the ongoing process of defining a coherent self.

A third group of theorists (8) that Miller discusses view shame as a response to any situation that the individual judges to be evidence of personal failure. It is an acute feeling of inferiority that involves any aspect of the self or the whole self.

A situation judged as a failure can be related to one's failure to move forward developmentally. The individual is believed to have succumbed to regressive desires. For example, the 21-year-old college graduate who has setbacks in acquiring professional employment and leaving her family to establish her own place of residence experiences the same shame as does the four-year-old who soils his pants.

Interpersonally Based Shame

Gershen Kaufman, in his book, *Shame: The Power Of Caring* (9), states that shame originates interpersonally, particularly within the nexus of a significant relationship. He links shame dynamically to a failure by a significant other person to respond appropriately to the individual's needs.

According to Kaufman (10), shame is activated when one significant person breaks the "interpersonal bridge" with another. Interpersonal bridge is defined as the emotional bond that ties two individuals together. This bond involves trust and allows for experiences of vulnerability and openness between individuals. It also becomes the catalyst for mutual understanding, change and personal growth. Consequently, emotional disruption of the interpersonal bridge has the most significant potential for inducing shame.

The shame-inducing process takes place whenever one's needs are not responded to appropriately by a significant other. (10) This failure to respond can occur in benign ways or more destructive ways. The destructive responses involve disparagement, humiliation, ridicule or some transfer of blame. Although we cannot always meet the needs of people we value or love, we can acknowledge or communicate that we understand and recognize the need. According to Kaufman, "Responding appropriately entails having the need understood and openly acknowledged whether or not it is gratified." (11)

As an experience, shame can be felt and then dissipate. Internalized shame, however, is the process whereby shame is prolonged for an indefinite period of time. When the shame experience becomes internalized, the individual can feel shame even when it is not induced by an interpersonal event. Interpersonally induced shame then becomes internally induced shame. (10)

The internalization of shame can occur at any point in our lives because we are constantly in the process of defining who we are through our interactions with others. Though we believe that the rupturing of the interpersonal bridge is a primary factor in the development of internalized shame, we also believe that the more generalized expectations of a shame-based culture can augment the internalized shame process.

The need for relationship, to belong, is a basic need for all of us. To be in a consistent, nurturing, reciprocal relationship fosters a sense of connectedness, a bond. As the bond begins to strengthen and mature, each person increasingly demonstrates a sense of caring and valuing of the other.

According to Kaufman (10), shame can be generated if this bond or connection is severed or disrupted. This split occurs whenever a need is not responded to or acknowledged. For example, a wife expresses her need for more time with her husband. His response is to tell her that she shouldn't need him so much, that as an adult, she should be more self-sufficient. This interaction can generate shame in the wife since her need for intimacy was rebuffed. She will feel shame for needing her husband and rage at his rejection.

If the bond can be mended or restored, then the shame-inducing experience can be healed. Let's go back to our husband and wife. Let's say that after a few moments the husband realizes that he was irritable with his wife because he was preoccupied with a job-related stressor. He tells her that he didn't mean to be so short with her and apologizes for his insensitivity. They then discuss her need for more time with him and work out a compromise. The bond or balance in the relationship has been restored and the couple has reached an agreement that will foster more intimate time together.

If there are shame experiences where the bonding has been disrupted and no effort to re-establish it has been made, the individual develops a sense of alienation and the feeling of not being good enough. Continued emotional separations or rifts promote a shame-trait or shame-based identity.

According to Kaufman (10), the phenomenology of shame is a feeling whereby the individual feels "seen in a painfully diminished sense." The sudden, unexpected exposure is what characterizes the basic nature of the shame experience. Shame is the awareness that we are painfully deficient or lacking as a human being. One of the most significant secondary reactions which can follow the shame experience is anger/rage.

When rage follows the shame experience, it serves to insulate and protect the self against any further exposure and also serves to alienate others by keeping them away so as to avoid feeling the shame. The shame/rage cycle can be crippling to relationships unless there is a restoration of the affectional tie. (10)

Shame And Identity

Every individual is faced with the questions, *Who am I?* and *Where do I fit in?* The need to belong is a basic human need and, according to Kaufman (12), identification (discovering who I am through the process of belonging) is the base of a personal sense of rootedness. The identification process begins first within the family, followed by the peer group and social institutions. Differentiation, that which makes us different from our family and others, is an alternating process which also aids the individual in developing the definition of self.

According to Kaufman (12), identification begins visually with the child watching and imitating the behaviors of those people who are most important to her. As the child's cognitive and emotional capabilities expand, simple modeling is expanded to include what Kaufman describes as imagery. (12) The child begins to integrate what she observes as a part of her internal definition of herself. She imagines she is like that part of mother or father she has been observing. "Imagery provides the bridge from outer to inner and enables the child to experience himself as a part of father or a part of mother." (13) Kaufman believes we internalize both good and bad identification images.

A child identifies with those individuals who hold absolute power over her life. Her personal identity is the result of the process of identification. According to Kaufman, internalization is the link through which identification actually leads to identity development. Identity development involves three separate dimensions (12):

1. Individuals internalize specific feelings, beliefs and attitudes about themselves from what significant others say.
2. Individuals internalize the manner in which they are treated by significant others.

3. Individuals internalize identifications in the form of images which are generally unconscious but which are taken inside and made their own.

The case of Brigit is a good example of how these three dimensions work together to formulate a sense of self.

Brigit, a 38-year-old compulsive overeater, was the oldest of five children in a family she described as always working hard to be successful. Her parents were young and had very definite ideas about how their children would act and what they would do with their lives.

Brigit did not measure up to their expectations. A curious and physically active child, she remembers being frequently reprimanded by her mother for not being more ladylike and for getting her playclothes dirty. Upon entering elementary school, she seemed to always receive demerits from her teachers for not being able to sit still and be quiet. She had difficulty learning to read and was soon labeled a slow learner. Her grades were always borderline passing.

Her parents were deeply disappointed. To make matters worse, Brigit's younger sister possessed all the qualities that Brigit did not. "Why can't you be more like Betts?" her mother would ask. "She is such a good student and involved in so many activities at school. All you ever want to do is watch television. I don't understand what your problem is. I just can't believe that you don't have the brains. After all, your father and I are both college grads and we never had any academic deficiencies." Not only did her parents complain, her teachers would say, "You are not smart enough to take college prep courses." She even remembers overhearing one of her teachers in high school tell her mother that there was no hope for Brigit and that they, her parents, would be lucky to have her graduate from high school.

Early in her life, Brigit remembers being angry and unhappy with herself. She not only felt badly about disappointing her parents and teachers but she felt as though she were really a bad person, as though there were something drastically wrong with her. She tried to be more like her mother and her sister in her actions and her interests but never felt that she measured up in comparison to them. It seemed that no matter what she did, her mother either corrected it or compared it to Betts. She was angry but believed her teachers' assessment of her lack of intelligence and consequently never tried courses or activities that she deemed too advanced for her, even though she might be genuinely interested in the subject. Though she did manage to finish high school, she always viewed herself as dumb.

Brigit's identity was built on her parents' feelings of disappointment and frustration, on being compared to her sister and on her teachers' assessment of her academic abilities and motivational deficiencies. In treatment, Brigit frequently would call herself stupid and compare her lack of progress to others in the group. When she participated in a guided imagery exercise designed to help patients get more in touch with their views and perceptions of themselves, she described her image of herself as a "large, lifeless mass of nothing."

She consistently demeaned herself for being "just a mother" and panicked when group members suggested she go back to school or look for work outside the home. Brigit saw herself and treated herself as a failure as had her parents and teachers.

Shame And Motivational Systems

In addition to the identity process previously discussed, Kaufman sees human beings as having three motivational systems which can be additional contributing sources to the shame internalization process: affects or feelings, drives and needs. (12) Shame can be generated in any of these systems and, undetected, can eventually prevent people from being able to acknowledge or express their feelings, drives or needs because of the shame associated with them. Kaufman refers to these as shame binds. (12)

Affect Shame Binds

Whenever a feeling — anger, joy, fear — is met with a response from a significant other that induces shame, an affect shame bind may result. An affect shame bind serves to control the later expression of the feeling involved.

Lissa, a 29-year-old bulimic, vividly remembers that when she was about 11, someone stole a ring that a boy had given her. She ran home, crying about the lost ring. Instead of acknowledging her feelings, her mother met her at the door with, "Why are you so upset? It was only a cheap ring anyway. Besides, you are late. Where have you been?" Lissa remembers initially being startled by her mother's reaction and then she recalls that she screamed at her mother to shut up. Then she ran down the street and hid in the park. When she was found, she was severely reprimanded and sent to her room, where she cried herself to sleep.

Lissa expressed anger to her mother because of the shame she felt in being yelled at and ridiculed in response to her deep feelings of sadness. Since then, Lissa has had difficulty expressing her anger in intimate relationships.

For compulsive eaters, particularly women, a major affect shame bind centers on the affect of interest or excitement. Silvan Tomkins (14), a noted feelings theorist, delineates seven basic affects: interest-excitement, enjoyment-joy, surprise-startle, distress-anguish, anger-rage, fear-terror and shame-humiliation. The interest-excitement affect is the most frequently experienced human emotion. It provides the motivation for learning, creativity and the acquisition of skills. The subjective experience of interest involves an attentiveness, curiosity and fascination with the object. Interest is zest, excitement, curiosity.

The curiosity and exploratory behaviors of little girls, however, is stifled by gender-specific prohibitions. Although a mother may encourage crawling and walking for her daughter, she will, at some point, lessen her enthusiasm for ongoing physical independence because of social expectations of what's safe and acceptable for a female child.

We will talk later about how this relates to body image more fully. However, for our purposes now, it's important to note that exploratory feelings in little girls are often shame-bound due to the culture's need to see females as passive, which translates into the mother's need to protect the female child more than the male child.

Lissa has a vague recollection of wanting to climb a tree when she was about four years old. She had seen her older brother do it. The big old oak tree fascinated her with its gnarled roots protruding from the earth and its rich foliage seen against the sky. She remembers being so curious about what was up there. As she began to climb the majestic tree, her mother saw her from the kitchen and pounded on the window, screaming frantically. She ran out and grabbed Lissa by the arm. "Don't you ever try to do that again. What is wrong with you? You stay close to the house where I can keep an eye on you."

Lissa's curiosity about the world around her was met with anger and criticism. Lissa, like most young girls, probably felt a sense of shame at her curiosity, her interest in exploring. Women often feel awkward or self-conscious if they think they have gone beyond the boundaries of what is acceptable.

Drive - Shame Binds

Human drives include hunger, thirst and sex. Kaufman (12) focuses on the drive - shame bind of sex and sees that the sex drive is the one most associated with shame. Although we agree with Kaufman, we feel he has ignored a drive - shame bind that is critically significant to the shame experienced by women, that of hunger. This will be explored more fully later. Suffice it to say that for compulsive eaters there is a great deal of shame connected with their hunger but this hunger goes beyond the physical sensation and becomes associated with the hunger for connectedness, for reciprocal relationships.

Kaufman does say that as bodily responses fail to measure up to self-imposed standards, exposure deepens and shame increases. (12) Compulsive eaters often perceive their hunger as overpowering and insatiable. Hunger is viewed with contempt and is often seen as the enemy, the culprit that interferes with the compulsive eater's desire to be in control and to rise above her basic needs.

Interpersonal Needs Shame Binds

According to Kaufman, drives and affects (feelings) are not sufficient to comprise a comprehensive motivational understanding of human development. Forming and maintaining reciprocal relationships is a key factor in human maturation. Shame can be internalized when a person's attempt to have an interpersonal need met is thwarted or unacknowledged.

Kaufman identifies six basic elements to the interpersonal need system (12):

1. The need for a relationship in which an individual feels loved and wanted as a person is the most fundamental need. Shame results when a child fails to experience such a relationship.
2. The need for touching or holding is a biologically based need and allows the individual to feel safe, comfortable and protected. Shame results when the kind and quality of touch is withholding or abusive.
3. The need for identification and the desire to be like the parent allows the parent to transmit and the child to receive what Kaufman refers to as a "personal culture." (12) Shame results not only from inconsistencies in what the parent says and does but also from any secrecy or withdrawal on the part of a parent.
4. The need for differentiation is one whereby the individual feels she has a separate identity. Separation is seen as a vital aspect of human development. Shame results from parental overprotectiveness and overpossessiveness. When parents resist physical, emotional or cognitive autonomy on the part of the child, the child may experience a deep sense of shame for being different.
5. The need to nurture is defined as one in which the child wants to be allowed to give nurturance rather than just receiving it. Shame results when her attempts to nurture a significant adult are rejected, ridiculed or ignored.

6. The need for affirmation is the need to be valued and to feel worthwhile. This affirming process is initially developed through significant others but eventually the individual must learn how to self-affirm. Shame results from nonacceptance. The child who has never felt truly accepted by her parents will have a difficult time affirming and accepting herself.

Most developmental theorists, Kaufman included, see the process of human emotional development as occurring in successive stages, with the ultimate goal being a sense of separation of self from others. For decades, theorists have believed that a person must have a distinct sense of separateness and disconnection from others before she can engage in healthy, intimate adult relationships.

Though we concur with the interpersonal needs concept outlined by Kaufman, we disagree that separation is the most vital aspect of human development. This point of view, in and of itself, generates more shame, particularly for women. By calling separation the ultimate goal of development, we believe people are encouraged to see their ongoing need for interpersonal closeness as a sign of weakness and to place a label of inferiority on those who recognize this need in themselves. This is a major self-shame theme for compulsive eaters.

The Masculine As Universal

Traditional psychological theories of development are based on a culturally-altered, masculine perception of the world. These theories have tended to view psychological development as a system of separating the self emotionally from the primary caretaker. A sense of self — an inner sense of being an individual — occurs in time. This separation process takes place through a sequence of emotional crises that, upon successful resolution, leave the person with somewhat more of a sense of self, a self that is more emotionally developed, more self-sufficient.

These views have been solely based on a masculine perspective of psychological development. Recently, several writers (15) have postulated that there are very real and important sex differences in the experience and construction of the self.

Carol Gilligan, in her book, *In A Different Voice*, says, " . . . Implicitly adopting the male life as the norm, they (psychological theorists) have tried to fashion women out of a masculine cloth. It all goes back, of course, to Adam and Eve — a story which shows, among other things, that if you make a woman out of a man, you are bound to get into trouble. In the life cycle as in the Garden of Eden, the woman has been the deviant. The penchant of developmental theorists to project a masculine image and one that appears frightening to women, goes back at least to Freud." (16)

Perhaps traditional theories regarding the separation/individuation process need to be re-examined. These theories have been greatly influenced by our cultural bias to use the masculine experience as universal.

Gender Identity Formation

Nancy Chodorow (17, 18) postulates that gender identity formation is very different for boys and girls. These differences, according to Chodorow, are not due to physiology but rather to the fact that women are mainly responsible for child care.

Given the fact that the primary caretaker for all children is typically female for at least the first three years, the interpersonal dynamics of gender identity formation is different for boys and girls. Gender identity for girls takes place within the context of the ongoing relationship between mother and daughter. Mothers experience daughters as *like* themselves. Conversely, daughters experience themselves as *like* their mothers, thus bonding the experience of attachment with identity formation. Boys, on the other hand, in defining themselves as masculine must *separate* themselves from their mothers and each views the other as an "other."

Gilligan (16) concludes that relationships and dependency issues are experienced very differently by men and women. Separation/individuation from mother is critical for the development of masculinity whereas femininity is defined through attachment. According to Gilligan, "Male gender identity is threatened by intimacy, while female gender identity is threatened by separation. Thus, males tend to have difficulty with relationships, while females tend to have problems with individuation." (17, 18)

This is much more than a descriptive difference. It creates strong feelings of inadequacy and shame for women who have been expected to develop psychologically like men. The need for relationship becomes a liability for women and is viewed as a failure to develop appropriately.

It is important to note that the lack of recognition of the female experience as different and acceptable has a direct impact on shame formation for compulsive eaters.

This need for affiliation, often viewed as a weakness, has become shame-bound and, as we have mentioned, it has become symbolically connected to the physical drive of hunger.

Marissa often describes herself as weak and needy. "It seems as though I need to be attached to someone all the time. What is wrong with me?" she asks in desperation. "I can't tolerate being angry with anyone I'm close to. I feel so alone, so disconnected whenever there is a rift. I can't tolerate the distance. Whenever I have an argument with my husband, or my mother, or whoever, I am the first one to make up and say I'm sorry. It makes me angry that I'm so damned needy. I binge a lot when I feel someone is upset with me. I should be more independent. I know if I could just control my eating and if I were thinner, I wouldn't be so affected by the way other people treat me. It's just one more thing about myself I feel ashamed of," she says as she pounds her fist on the arm of her chair.

In therapy, we have tried to help Marissa develop an appreciation for her relational needs and to transform her thinking about dependence and neediness from a negative to a positive valence. This transformation includes helping her to take more responsibility for herself as a partner in a relationship.

Self-In-Relation Theory

The Stone Center at Wellesley College has been focusing its research attention on the psychological development of women and has defined the self-in-relation model of development. "The notion of the self-in-relation makes an important shift in emphasis from separation to relationship as the basis for self-experience and development. Further, relationship is seen as the basic goal of development, that is, the deepening capacity for relationship and relational competence. The self-in-relation model assumes that other aspects of self, e.g. creativity, autonomy, assertion, develop within this primary context. That is, other aspects of self-development emerge in the context of relationship, and **there is no inherent need to disconnect or to sacrifice relationship for self-development**." (19)

What this new model emphasizes is that the degree or direction of growth is not toward more autonomy and the severing of early emotional ties but rather toward a process of growth within the relationship wherein both individuals are encouraged to maintain the connection and to be flexible and adaptable to the change of growth in the other.

Development takes place through a more expanded and acknowledged relational experience. "For example, the adolescent does not necessarily want to separate from her parents, but to change the form and content of the relationship in a way that affirms her own developmental changes and allows new relationships to develop and take priority. If this important need to continue the relationship but also to change in the relationship is not honored, both daughters and mothers will feel shame and diminished self-worth." (20) Our cultural expectation for "healthy" emotional development makes people feel unable to separate and therefore "unhealthy" when that is not what they want or need.

Baker Miller and like-minded theorists suggest, essentially, that the ultimate purpose of psychological development is not autonomy or separation and individuation as we have come to know these principles. Nor is psychological development a linear, hierarchical process. Psychological development for all human beings is, however, what has come to be labeled in our culture as more "feminine" in that it is fundamentally based in and occurring through the process of affiliation. In other words, psychological development is an ongoing process in the human experience of varying affiliations that never ends.

Certainly there are unhealthy dependencies, more recently labeled as "co-dependency" in relationships but we need to develop a new baseline for what this really means.

Co-dependency And Healthy Affiliation

Co-dependency is generally defined as a result of an individual's failure to psychologically separate and develop an autonomous self (21) in early childhood. This affects all subsequent relationships. It is characterized by the following:

- lack of trust in self and others.
- low self-esteem.
- feeling trapped in relationships.
- feeling addicted to and powerless because of another.
- needing strong and continuous affirmation and approval from others.
- feeling unable to set limits and face conflicts for fear of abandonment.
- inability to verbally express feelings and needs.
- magical thinking including wanting others to automatically know and understand feelings and needs and expecting the same from self.

The belief that co-dependency is based on an individual's failure to become independent and to separate fosters feelings of shame regarding our basic human need for relationship. Frequently when patients in treatment begin to learn and read about co-dependency, they feel a great sense of shame for not being "strong enough" or "independent enough" in their primary relationships. Concurrently, they also express a fear that to be a healthier partner in a relationship means to be unaffected by the other's feelings and behaviors and not to need or depend on the other person for support or for validation of any kind. It is easy to fall into the trap of believing that they should be able to be emotionally fulfilled and secure totally by and within themselves.

This belief, based on the masculine experience of psychological development, discounts the importance of relationship as an ongoing, fluid process. Rather than seeing co-dependency as a failure to separate, we believe that co-dependency is based on the individual's inability to function maturely within the relationship. This maturity is based on reciprocal mutuality where the needs of both individuals are valued and appreciated. Growth occurs within the context of an ever changing relationship.

The early mother-child relationship is a mutual exchange through which both individuals develop an increased sense of self. The early mother-child relationship has been traditionally viewed as the core, therefore the most influential relationship, in the child's developing sense of self. Historically, mothers have been blamed for all the child's later emotional difficulties. The mother may not have been nurturing enough or consistent enough in fulfilling the child's needs. This sets parents and children up to believe in the notion of perfectionism, that if a mother truly loves her child, she will be able to anticipate and fulfill *all* of the child's needs. This expectation then becomes the yardstick by which not only the mother-child relationship but all relationships are measured.

It is true that the primary caretaker of an infant and young child is fundamental in the child's developing a sense of self and learning how to relate to others. However, much of the infant and early childhood development research currently being conducted (22) indicates that infants, rather than being passive receptacles to be formed solely by their caretakers, begin life with primitive abilities to engage and interact with others. What is being discovered is that the caretaker's responsiveness does stimulate the child and the child's responsiveness also stimulates the caretaker in a feedback loop. This is not to say that adults in an adult-child relationship are less responsible for their interactions with the child or in providing the child with the supportive environment necessary to grow and develop. However, what it does allow for is recognition of both the child and the adult as people rather than as objects with varying levels of emotional, physical and social needs and skills. The interaction they share must be responsive to their individual needs, yet flexible enough to change in the ongoing relationship as these individuals grow, mature and change.

Co-dependency results when an individual cannot find ways to allow relationships to grow beyond the idealized, early parent-child relationship. Co-dependency occurs when the individual cannot give up the fantasy that the other person is there solely to take care of all of her physical and emotional needs and vice versa. The individual's dilemma is not based in her inability to separate but rather in her inability to function at a mutual, empathic and reciprocal level. Rather than focusing on the dependency, the need for relationship (which fuels shame) as the culprit in the development of co-dependency, we see the inability to negotiate and delineate varying kinds of relationships and levels of mutuality and reciprocity as a major contributor. These negotiations should encompass the emotional, social, physical and spiritual needs of both adult and child. Dawn and her mother, Alice, are an excellent example of the need to negotiate change in a parent-child relationship.

Alice, a 42-year-old single parent, sought treatment for the severe conflicts she was having with her 16-year-old daughter, Dawn, who was the youngest of four children and the only one still living at home. They engaged in frequent screaming matches about Dawn's emerging need to develop relationships outside of the family.

Alice would say, "It's as though she has become another person. This is not the girl I used to know. Dawn used to be so loving and affectionate. We used to be so close. Ever since she started high school, I began to notice a change in her. I just don't know what has happened to her. If I didn't know better, I would think she was on drugs. All she is interested in is her friends, her appearance and boys. She is on the phone a lot and stays in her room during the week. On weekends, I rarely get to see her. Now that she has her driver's license, I never see her. As a matter of fact, we have been fighting more and more since she has been driving."

Alice recognizes that Dawn needs to have friends and activities of her own but she can't shake the anger she generally feels toward Dawn. "There is a part of me that knows she needs to begin a life of her own but there is another part that feels alone and abandoned. I never realized how much I depended on her to meet my need for companionship. I feel so ashamed of the part of me that can't let her go," she says, tears welling up in her eyes.

Dawn reports feeling very guilty at leaving her mother alone with no one to talk to and ashamed for being so selfish. "Even though I leave the house really pissed off, I feel awful. While my friends are having a great time, I smile and pretend to be having fun but I am really feeling awful about my mom. I feel sorry for her but I get so damned mad at her. I am not doing anything bad or wrong. I just want to have fun and be with my friends. Why does she react so? "

This is an excellent example of a relationship that is stuck and still operating in an earlier stage of development. While Dawn, developmentally, needs to include other people and activities in her life, Alice is still trying to maintain an exclusive mutual mother-child relationship. Alice's inability to allow her relationship with Dawn to integrate the developmental changes that are necessary for Dawn's growth, leaves Dawn feeling that she has to choose between meeting her own needs versus meeting her mother's. Dawn, experiencing her own struggle with emerging independence, is also having difficulty integrating the change in the relationship with her mother. There are times when Dawn wants to be treated like an adult and there are times she wants to be taken care of by her mother. This confuses Alice and reinforces her belief that Dawn needs her to be the mother she has always been. It sets the stage for a potential co-dependent relationship.

What is not happening is the acceptance and recognition by both Dawn and Alice that, while relationships may change, they do not necessarily end. They are both afraid that they will no longer need each other if Dawn becomes the emancipated, independent person she should be. This fear interrupts the life development stages of both. While Dawn needs to develop relationships and activities apart from her family, Alice also needs to rely less on her daughter and to expand her own world, since her role as a mother is changing. This change in the relationship requires both Dawn and Alice to negotiate and tolerate changes in the form and content of the relationship so that both of them can feel affirmed and connected. Dawn does not need or want to separate from her mother. She simply wants to be able to interact with her mother in a more adult fashion. Alice's fear that change means separation causes her to hang on to Dawn more tightly. This makes Dawn want to pull away so that Alice's fears are, in fact, realized. Through treatment, Dawn and her mother were able to verbalize their fears about the change that was occurring in their relationship and at the same time to negotiate ways of accepting their individual needs and feelings.

The goal with our patients is to help them reframe their one-sided masculine view of relationships as always resulting in separation and disconnection with significant others by encouraging them to develop an appreciation of their feminine, relational needs and to see these as a strength. As a result, much of their fear, guilt and shame is diminished. It's all right to need others — actually, it is essential for a deeper, more enriched life.

Beyond Shame

The more recently developed theories regarding shame and addiction tend to focus on its development in the context of interpersonal relationships. Although we support the basic tenets of these theories, there is a critical omission which makes it difficult to fully understand the shame experience for the compulsive eater. This omission focuses on our culture's role in shame formation.

Our culture is based on patriarchal principles which foster separation between God and man and man within himself. Patriarchy is a hierarchal system espousing the superiority and dominance of white males as a ruling group. The female perspective has been devalued.

Rather than viewing life from a holistic stance where the masculine and feminine work in harmony, our culture fosters an adversarial relationship between the two. A deep sense of shame has been created, not only for women who believe they are innately inferior but for all individuals who demonstrate more feminine qualities and values.

The inferiority of the feminine has been a major factor in shame formation. Eating disorders symbolize the struggle men and women face in their attempts to become less ashamed of what they perceive as their weak, inferior side.

Recovery from eating disorders involves embracing rather than denying our feminine side. Even though our culture has viewed the feminine as inferior and weak, recovering individuals must recognize the inherent strength of both the feminine and the masculine operating as partners or as two aspects of the same whole rather than as separate and distinct entities.

In the next chapter we will explore these concepts more fully.

Shame And The Compulsive Eater

In our work with eating disorder patients, we have discovered that their greatest shame initially centers around their bodies and their relationship with food. This relationship encompasses the consumption of food and the rituals around food preparation, obsessive meal planning, purging, exercise, dieting, weight and body image.

Food as an addictive substance has a special meaning in the shame experience because of its association with physical hunger and effects on the body, as well as its association with emotional neediness and the desire for connectedness with others.

Food And Hunger

Food symbolizes relationship and survival. Food and eating ensure the survival of the infant and also begin the process of interpersonal relating. Feeding becomes a shared, pleasurable and emotionally satisfying experience for both the mother and infant. The intensity of this relationship changes as the infant becomes more and more self-sufficient. However, food continues to be a primary way in which the mother nurtures the child. For the child, food and mother become inextricably linked.

As we grow up, food and eating continue to provide us with comfort, nurturance and intimacy. Food does more than nourish the body; it has come to symbolize nurturance, security, safety and love, all of which are associated with the mother figure. We often reach out for food when, in fact, we are not experiencing physical hunger. We may be feeling lonely, uncared for, angry or frightened and we seek out food as a way to be mothered through these feelings.

When this primary feeding relationship is dysfunctional, the basic need for a reciprocal emotional relationship is disrupted. A greater dependency on food to meet this need is likely to develop. We discussed this in our book, *Feeding the Empty Heart.* (23)

For the compulsive eater, addiction to food is a constant reminder of the individual's neediness, which actually transcends the food itself. It encompasses the need for others, the need to be nurtured and loved. However, in a culture that values individualism and control and negates emotion and relationships, this hunger fuels deep feelings of shame which we refer to as selfshame.

Selfshame is based on our inability to control our hunger. This hunger, more than just physical in nature, encompasses our need to be needed, our need to need and the full range of our emotions.

The compulsive eater's selfshame is threefold. The selfshame is rooted in the inability to control physical need for food, inability to control the existence of emotions, and inability to forego need for interpersonal relationships.

Food And The Body

By today's cultural standards, fleshiness is viewed as a sign of weakness, a perspective of femininity which narrowly includes matronliness, dependency, emotionality and passivity. A lean, angular body is preferred and has become a symbol of control, independence and power. When a women succumbs to her "hungers," she fears her weaknesses will be exposed by her body's size and shape.

The world will see through her and discover that she is dependent and needy. By control of her body, she desperately attempts to hide her selfshame. Attempting to control body size and shape is a way to hide the need for others.

However the female body, due to its reproductive capacities, is naturally soft, round and fleshy, particularly in the thighs, buttocks, abdomen and breast. The twentieth century woman is placed in a dilemma, both physically and emotionally. The body she feels she has to create in order to hide her selfshame is in conflict with her biological nature. Her natural relational needs are in conflict with the culture's emphasis on individualism and the masculine perspective on separation/individuation.

Bodyshame grows out of selfshame. It is based on our struggle to control our feminine nature, which includes the physical need for nourishment, the emotional need for connectedness and the biological form of the female body. Consumed with bodyshame, compulsive eaters are trying to make the female body and femininity fit into a mold which goes against their very nature.

We live in a culture that values control — power over — which means that any form of control is good, simply because it *is* a control. Its value lies in its existence rather than in what it accomplishes or creates.

Women are faced with a dilemma. They have been assigned the task of providing nurturance to others in the form of food, empathy, support, etc. However, they must keep their own need for nurturance in check.

In a culture that values control, we are supposed to be able to manage our needs and drives. Food and physical hunger are a reminder that no matter how much control we attain, we will always be connected to nature and/or limited human capacities.

Kim Chernin, in her book, *The Obsession* (24), says that a woman's desire to control her hunger may express the fact that she has been socialized to view her emotional life, her feelings, desires and needs as dangerous and therefore needing control and careful monitoring.

Control over the inner self becomes a way to feel powerful and successful. Being independent, strong and rational seem to be the goal to achieve. This becomes particularly important as women enter the male marketplace, if they are to succeed.

Fat comes to symbolize a failure to achieve, viewed as a sign of weakness, dependency, emotionality. Hunger and the body are the enemy. Shame, bodyshame and selfshame, inextricably entwined in that the fleshy body reveals a defective, needy inner self, a self that is weak, dependent and out of control. This fleshy, heavy body absorbs the inner shame and the individual begins to develop a belief system that says, *If I could only lose weight, I would be in control, successful and happy.* Bodyshame is the receptacle for the selfshame. As long as the individual can focus on weight and physical hunger as the problem, then she does not have to feel the shame of her emotional needs to their full intensity.

Thus, for the food addicted person, shame is a dual experience — selfshame and bodyshame. Shame about the self for loss of control is transformed not only into the compulsive behavior (selfshame as a result of a lack of control) but is also transferred onto the body.

In this chapter, we have briefly discussed the various psychological theories of shame and we have concurred essentially with the belief that unhealthy shame results from disruptions in the interpersonal bridge between significant individuals. When this rupture is longstanding or occurs repeatedly, the shame becomes internalized and part of the individual's self-identity. This shaming occurs through a combination of the way the individual is treated and talked about by her role models, the attitudes and expectations conveyed by her role models and the way these significant others handle her feelings, drives and needs.

However, beyond the significance of these interpersonal relationships, we believe that another major shaming element in the individual's developing self-concept is the culture. The culture transmits beliefs, values and attitudes through its major institutions such as the family. Our culture has transmitted beliefs which, among other things, create a sense of shame regarding the basic human need (though traditionally viewed as a feminine quality) of affiliation.

Because this need is seen as a sign of weakness, it is deplored. Men and women feel ashamed of it and attempt to hide it but because one of women's gender myth characteristics is to be nurturing and caretaking, many women feel they are in a double bind. They are asked to be something that relegates them to an inferior position. Bodyshame is often the result of trying to find a way to achieve the idealized image of control through the shape of their body and consequently to hide the inner need of affiliation.

In the next chapter, we will discuss the culture's general role in shame formation as it relates to the shaming of the feminine and of the female body in particular.

3

Shame, Culture And The Female Body

The Culture's Role In Shame Formation

The culture is a primary teacher and therefore a contributor to the development of shame in its members. A culture develops within a social group and includes the customary beliefs, social norms and material traits of a specific religious, racial or social group. (1) The culture becomes the means through which its members attempt to understand life in general and its individual members' roles specifically. In our own country, we have many religious and ethnic cultures (Jewish, Hispanic, Black, Amish) but we also have an overall culture which is transmitted through the legal system, the media, the public education system and our economic system.

Sociologists, social anthropologists and philosophers generally believe that the way in which a culture views life can be defined within two major perspectives. The labels for these perspectives vary. Some say a culture is either nomadic or earth-cultivating (2); either domination-oriented or affiliative (3); either progressive and historical or traditional and nonhistorical (4); either patriarchal or matriarchal.

In this discussion of culture and its role in shame formation, we will be exploring the two major perspectives from the point of view of what we refer to as the hierarchical system and the affiliative system.

A hierarchical system is commonly referred to as patriarchal and is also associated with being nomadic, domination-oriented, progressive and historical. The affiliative system is commonly referred to as the feminine system (though not necessarily matriarchal) and is generally associated with earth-cultivating, traditional and nonhistorical systems.

Whether a culture is hierarchical or affiliative influences all areas of an individual's life. However, what is most significant in exploring shame formation is how the culture views its members' relationship with a Higher Power/Nature and the interrelationships among its members.

The Hierarchical Framework

Within the hierarchical framework man is separated from God/Nature and needs to do something to become one with God/Nature again. Spiritually, this is the ultimate disruption in the interpersonal bridge and becomes the basis of perfectionism. Shame results from feeling disconnected. Because man feels disconnected from God/Nature, from his basic wholeness, he continually seeks to re-establish the bond by controlling and transcending his human nature (his emotions, needs, drives and body) and by attempting to exercise control over nature in general.

In hierarchical (patriarchal) cultures, God tends to be viewed as an artist. (5) When a culture sees God strictly as an artist, as in the Genesis story of the creation of man from the dust of the earth, God is seen as separate and capable of objective, sometimes harsh, criticism of His creation. Consequently, the God-as-artist has the capacity to destroy creation at any time if He perceives that His creation doesn't live up to His standards and expectations. When a human is seen as the artistic creation of God, then life comes from the Divine Word.

In this instance, the flesh — the human body — is not seen as sacred. In fact, it is frequently viewed as something that imprisons the spirit and is a roadblock to perfection. The human body, then, is labeled as the source of all human weakness. In the extreme, the human body can even be seen as evil, demonic. Because it cannot be part of the divinity, it becomes its opposite. As philosopher Alan Watts says so eloquently, "The body, grudgingly admitted to be good because it is God's handiwork, has, in practice, been viewed as territory captured by the devil, and the study of human nature has been mostly the study of its foibles." (6)

Most of the philosophies of the West have been concerned with man's desire for a stable, unchanging state of existence in which he has ultimate control. (5) Since man can't control nature, can't control drought or flood for example, he rectifies this by saying he has dominion over nature. This sets the stage for a conflict or oppositional way of looking at man's relationship with the natural world in all things associated with nature. Those who feel at home with the earth and rely upon the constancy of change and the transformations of life are negated by those who feel unable to accept the constancy, who seek changelessness and who eventually feel alienated, separated from nature. In hierarchical systems, being alienated from all natural things becomes the goal of spirituality. Life on the earth is not "real" life. Real life is perfect, incorruptible and unchanging. To be spiritual, then, is to transcend the natural world with all its changes, to minimize or repress human needs, drives, feelings, desires; and to hide and be ashamed of natural body processes and the body as a whole.

Anything, therefore, that tempts one to see the structure and goals of life differently is evil and must be controlled, negated or otherwise devalued. Here is the basis for our history's tendency to devalue earth-based cultures like those of certain American Indian tribes and to fear, demean and ridicule many of the natural female transformational processes such as menstruation, pregnancy and menopause.

Patriarchy or hierarchical systems are viewed in opposition to the affiliative or feminine system. The associations with patriarchy and the hierarchical system say that God is male and through His Word, life is created.

The ethics of the system are not based on affiliation but rather on abstract principles and rational thought. Reality and the value of life can be found only in the spiritual world. Death is seen as the way into the spiritual world, the highest form of existence. It is, essentially, living beyond nature. Time, in the hierarchical sense, is linear and ever moving toward that goal. The ultimate goal is to transcend nature in this world and, at death, to enter the perfection and changelessness of the spiritual world, heaven. (5)

In hierarchical systems, the feminine aspects of life in the symbolic sense and women in the literal sense have been associated with nature. Through this system, nature has been seen as something to be condemned and controlled. Consequently, females, the female body and femininity are also condemned and controlled.

Hierarchical cultures foster relationships that are based on competition. Power bases are clearly established with a one up-one down structure. An individual's place in the hierarchy determines how much power an individual can have via decision-making, ownership of property, etc. A hierarchical system uses comparisons among its members to maintain itself. Fear and judgments are used to keep people separated and distrustful of one another and therefore more compliant to the system. Women and the feminine principles are always kept in check and relegated to the "down" position.

The Affiliative Framework

Within the affiliative framework, on the other hand, individuals are in an ongoing relationship with God/Nature, which does not require repair and consequently there is no shame. Rather than striving for perfection, individuals are comfortable with their humanness and see themselves as a *part of* nature rather than *apart from* nature. This includes a full acceptance of their emotions, drives, needs and their bodies.

Often, in affiliative systems, God is seen as female or having many of the traditionally feminine characteristics. When God is seen as a mother, for example (5), the relationship between the creator and the creation becomes more clearly that between parent and child. In this framework, a human being is seen as godlike in both spiritual and physical forms because both come through the parent. A Mother-God provides comfort, protection, consolation and moral guidance. A Mother-God has more of an obligation to Her creation (humans), as the creation is a part of Her. Therefore, a Mother-God can also relate more closely to Her creation because She can see Herself in them.

In cultures where the image of God is as mother rather than artist, attitudes about the human body and sexuality are dramatically different from those held in the God-as-artist framework. When the creation is seen as something that was given birth to — therefore coming from and out of the body — the human body is viewed as holy, as divine — not evil. Sex becomes a sacred act, a holy obligation not a sign of evil or human weakness. (5)

It is believed that the affiliative system has its roots in the relationship between mother and child but is eventually expanded to include an entire value system, centered on being a part of, attached to and belonging to this world. In other words, the affiliative system sees human beings as belonging to and connected with nature and each other.

In an affiliative system, life is ever changing. Death occurs, life renews itself. There is neither control nor choice over these changes. The difficulty human beings have in accepting the constancy of change may have led to some of the fundamental beliefs of hierarchical systems.

In an affiliative system, God is female and all life comes from the female. The morals and ethics of life are based on blood ties. The world of nature is the model for all creation. Reality and the value of life can be found in the constant transformations which occur in the material world. Death terminates existence. Time is cyclical and life is based on the process of endless renewal. One finds the meaning of life by participating and sharing in human nature rather than by seeking to control and transcend it to achieve perfection. (5)

In an affiliative system, the members of the group are seen as equal; therefore, relationships are based on harmony and cooperation. Competition is unnecessary and power is evenly distributed.

Shame And The Feminine

Our primary cultures today are hierarchical and patriarchal in focus. Consequently the affiliative or feminine systems have been devalued and discounted. The masculine principle has been elevated to a superior position, leaving the feminine as inferior and subordinate.

Our culture emphasizes competition, winning, superiority and perfection. The elevation of these stereotypically masculine traits to the status of good, right and normal has resulted in the downgrading of the feminine traits. As our culture has become more civilized, the devaluing of the feminine has become more sophisticated and complex. It is hidden in our standards for morality, beauty and appearance, the female body and role expectations, as well as in our economic, legal, educational and religious institutions.

It is important to note that when we talk about the devaluing of the feminine, we are not simply talking about prejudice against women. All human beings have qualities and characteristics which can be defined in terms of masculine and feminine. For any human being to be whole, that individual must be able to understand, be comfortable with and utilize both the masculine and feminine aspects of himself or herself.

This concept of wholeness is based on the Chinese Tao Te Ching philosophy of the *yin* and the *yang* which believes that the feminine principle is not ruled by the masculine principle but rather that both work in concert with one another. Masculinity and femininity are not really opposites. They are instead different aspects of life which, through inter-relatedness, allow life to grow and continue. Leadership without cooperation, emotion without thought, creativity without action are shortlived and useless. Just as a piece of music needs melody and harmony, the interchange of flats, sharps and natural keys, of major and minor chords and refrains in order to be rich and spiritually moving, so also men and women need all of their capacities, both masculine and feminine, in order to feel whole as individuals. This allows for more meaningful, healthy relationships.

Dualism

Our culture espouses a predominantly masculine per-spective in its values and orientation which favors pro-ductivity, rationality and goal-orientation at the expense of the more interpersonal values traditionally recognized as feminine. This maintains the split which fuels a duality in our self-concepts. There is a part of ourselves that we must deny, reject, negate. In the process of denying, re-jecting or negating an aspect of ourselves, our sense of being fragments. We experience a sense of disconnected-ness and alienation. That is what we define as the collec-tive shame experience.

The spiritual "hole" created by our alienation from ourselves and from God/Nature is painful and frightening. Alcohol, food, starvation, sex, work, money become the tools we try to use to "fill it up." For those who have a biological predisposition to addictions and a dysfunctional family system, these tools may take on a life of their own. The collective shame these individuals experience becomes focused on to their relationship with an addictive sub-stance or activity.

The resolution to our collective shame is not to over-throw masculine principles and strictly reinstate only the feminine as "the Way, the Truth and the Light" but rather to embrace the feminine principles of nature, harmony, cooperation, contemplation, emotions, community, affec-tion, affiliation, sexuality and the like as simply different aspects of the whole. The whole also includes rational thought, energy in motion (action) and leadership (mas-culine principles). Seeing these as different aspects of one whole, we may allow ourselves to drop the need for power and control and help each other to reduce our shame at not living up to or being satisfied with the ideal images, as projected by the hierarchical system. The fem-inine will no longer be considered bad or wrong. It will simply be acknowledged as a different aspect of the whole.

The new psychology of women, the self-in-relation theory as proposed by Jean Baker-Miller, Carol Gilligan, Janet Surrey and others may be a healthy start to close the breach between man and woman and to heal the shame of our culture.

Rather than perpetuating the view of rugged individu-alism — *I don't need anyone and I can take care of myself* — we need to foster the concept of relationship — *I am a person in my own right and I cannot deny my need for a healthy connection with others.*

It is through our affiliations and endless interactions with others that we develop a sense of self and a sense of belonging. Both of these are necessary for us to feel whole.

Individuals who suffer from eating disorders tend to split off or deny their feminine sides, falling victim to the culture's dualism. They feel ashamed of their need for others and their inability to feel independent. They de-mean their relational needs and see these needs as weak and defective. They also feel ashamed of the body and its need for food, sex, rest and natural processes like aging. These natural human processes are instead viewed as proof of weakness, of loss of control and inferiority.

Consequently, such individuals strive to emulate mas-culine values only. Their goal is to have no feelings, to need no one and always to be in control. They are particularly victims of the hierarchical standard of perfectionism. The body has come to represent success or failure to the degree in which it adheres to this standard.

The Shaming Of The Female Body

Historical Roots

Given the female's reproductive capacities, the hierarchical system views the female body as closely associated with nature and therefore needing to be restrained and controlled.

According to Bryan S. Turner, author of *The Body and Society*, this control emerged from a need to safeguard a specific economic system. (7) In a hierarchical system, through both the subordination of women and the controls exercised over sexuality (and consequently over reproduction), men could more readily assure themselves of not only the accumulation of property but also the transference of property to their own heirs. This assured them of a place in the hierarchical system where accumulation of material things — land, sheep, money — were intricately interlinked with one's station in life.

Turner (7), therefore proposes that our current cultural attitudes toward femininity and the body are grounded both in the view of women as being too close to nature and in the economics of controlling property. By devaluing women and the human body, more control could be exercised over reproduction. The more control was exercised, the greater a man's chance of assuring that children born into his household were biologically his. His powerlessness to ensure paternity was dealt with by restricting women and sex and by relegating offspring to specific roles and classifications.

Even though the focus of controlling the female body is no longer on sex and reproduction, the hierarchical system continues to exert control over the female body in order to keep women in a "one down" position.

Today, consumerism is also a way to control the female body — we are constantly told that we need to look a certain way in order to be acceptable. Consumerism fosters our bodyshame by developing cosmetics, fashions and bodytypes which continually tell us that what we have is not good enough. As long as we are focused on the beautification of our bodies, we continue to accept the culture's denigration of the natural female body.

Women And Beauty

The identification of women with beauty has a long tradition in Western culture. Greeks associated men and women with different virtues; ambition was seen to be a male characteristic while beauty was a female quality. This association of women with beauty permeated 19th century art, philosophy, poetry and fiction. (8) Women are the good and the beautiful as well as the evil and the ugly — beauty and deviance.

Rita Freedman in *Beauty Bound* (9), discusses the dichotomy of masculinity and femininity. From this model, as we have been discussing, women are viewed as inferior to the masculine norm. How, then, can the female be honored as the "fair sex," beautiful and good — yet considered deeply inferior?

According to Freedman, " . . . myths about gender, like myths about beauty, are often linked in just such counterbalanced pairs. Together, contrary myths create an equilibrium that helps preserve them both. Women are crowned with beauty precisely because they are cloaked in difference. The idealization of female appearance camouflages an underlying belief in female inferiority . . . the myth of female beauty grows from the myth of female deviance. Beauty helps to balance woman as a misbegotten person. It disguises her inadequacies and justifies her presence." (10)

Freedman goes on to say that the reproductive role sets women apart from men and consequently is defined in relationship to their bodies. As we have discussed, motherhood connects women to nature allowing men to take ownership of the more sacred realm of culture. "Although assigned a separate and unequal place in society . . . woman cannot be exiled too far or too long . . . beauty confers added value on the devalued sex. It makes woman worthy of joining man's life, of sharing his bed, bearing his children, and wearing his name." (11)

Throughout the 19th century, beauty not only represented goodness and morality but it began to be equated with power. "Beauty represented neither morality nor goodness but rather a means of self-aggrandizement through admiration, homage and, ultimately, association with a powerful man. Woman was not only an Eve figure but also an individual obsessed with the self, with physical relationships with men, and with the eternal pursuit of beauty through whatever means." (12)

The female body has become an object of power, though that power is based on beauty. Lois Banner in *American Beauty* (8) differentiates between male and female power. Aggressive action is viewed as masculine and unfeminine. Beauty — not aggression or dominance — is the domain of woman. According to Banner, " . . . signals of power are confounded with signals of gender, creating a dominance hierarchy that rests on sex differences. As women learn to channel energy into being seen rather than into being strong, attracting becomes a substitute for acting." (13)

It is through their bodies that women function in the world and achieve status and recognition **if** they are thin enough and beautiful enough. It is difficult for us to maintain a sense of self and body as culturally acceptable and at the same time establish a sense of our own individuality. It is no wonder that our identity and self-esteem are deeply entwined with our body image.

Women and beauty have been historically identified with each other. Banner says, " . . . Americans viewed the preservation and inculcation of beauty, in addition to religion and spiritual values in general, as women's special concern." (14)

As a result of this obsession with our image, the body has become our slave. We are involved in a co-dependent, exploitative relationship with our bodies. We have come to believe that we can achieve a sense of harmony, peace or happiness by having the perfect body. The culture has fostered this obsessive pursuit and in doing so has fueled the shame we feel about our natural bodies.

Shame And The Female Body

Historical Roots

The beautification of the body and the pursuit of beauty appear to be a universal need and can be traced back to ancient civilizations. Many cultures have employed a variety of beautification rituals which actually involved mutilation of the female body and some of which appear grotesque to the Western world.

Chinese women bound their feet so as to appear fragile, delicate and dainty when walking. Their feet were bound so tightly that a natural high heel was formed. Toes were permanently twisted under the arch. As one woman recalls, "My footbinding began when I was seven with a ceremony on the lucky day of the month. That night, mother wouldn't let me remove the shoes. My feet felt on fire and I couldn't sleep . . . Beatings and curses were my lot for loosening the wrappings . . . Mother would remove the bindings and wipe the blood and pus which dripped from my feet. She said that only with the removal of the flesh could my feet become slender." (15)

Tribeswomen in Burma encircled their necks with so many heavy metal rings that their vertebrae would actually separate. African women used discs to form platypus lips. (16) In some tribes, clitoridectomies are performed on female infants. Equally grotesque are some of the devices that American women have subjected themselves to, improving an esthetically imperfect body by restricting their freedom and weakening their strength.

A good example is the corset, a standard item in a woman's wardrobe during the 19th century, when style dictated a waistline of 18 inches as ideal! Since this was virtually impossible naturally, women — desperate to conform — resorted to wearing corsets. The average corset exerted 21 pounds of pressure on a woman's internal organs and, in extreme cases, they actually measured up to 88 pounds of pressure. In addition, the fashionable woman wore an average of 37 pounds of street clothing in winter months, 19 pounds of which was suspended from her waist. The most immediate physiological reactions to this torture included shortness of breath, weakness and a propensity for violent indigestion. Longer term consequences were bent or fractured ribs, displacement of the liver and uterine prolapse. It has been documented that in some cases, the uterus would be gradually forced, by the pressure of the corset, out through the vagina. (17)

In the late 1860s the Grecian Bend became highly fashionable. "It involved the combination of a corset laced as tightly as possible with shoes having the highest possible heels in order to thrust the body both backward and forward, so that bosoms and buttocks would protrude as much as possible." (18) This style was so exaggerated that "women could not sit upright in carriages but rather had to lean forward and rest their hands on cushions on the floor."

In the early 20th century, influenced by French designer Paul Poiret, the corset was eliminated and replaced by the rubber girdle, to retract the hips. (19) The female body had to be restructured so as to make his designs look smoother.

After World War I, French designers continued to set the fashion standard and created the Flapper look. Women wore flattening brassieres constructed of shoulder straps and a single band of material that tightly encased the body from chest to waist. (19)

Besides devices to improve a woman's looks, there were cosmetics to add to beauty. Women have engaged in some bizarre rituals to achieve a certain type of look. During the Elizabethan age, women painted their faces white, using enamels made from egg whites or a mixture of vinegar and lead. Because the "natural" face was fashionable during the Victorian era, women avoided using these paints. However, some ate vinegar, chalk, even arsenic, in order to obtain a delicate, white complexion! (8)

While doing this research, we were amazed at what our female predecessors have done to look beautiful. Binding themselves in debilitating corsets, eating arsenic and flattening their breasts — all that seems a bit ridiculous. Binding the feet was barbaric. Yet, as we heighten our sensitivity to what we see as "normal" today, we realize that beautification strategies in the 1980s are just as masochistic and physically debilitating as they were a hundred years ago.

Dangerous Dieting

Perhaps the most significant event of the early 20th century was the first best-selling diet book, which promoted the belief that fat was definitely a liability. LuLu Hunt Peters, M.D., a Los Angeles physician, had a tremendous impact on values regarding dieting. She says, "Fat individuals have always been considered a joke . . . instead of being looked upon with friendly tolerance and amusement, you are now viewed with distrust, suspicion and even aversion."

She believed that dieting was as much related to the mind as it was to the body. She popularized calorie counting and thus was born the notion that natural body processes, appetite and body weight were under conscious control and that being overweight meant simply being out of control. This belief about overweight has remained entrenched in our values to this very day.

In the wake of World War I, women gained new social and political status. Cultural expectations about the body became more rigid. As more girls and women worked outside the home and attended colleges and universities, their sense of personal freedom together with a greater availability of choices promoted the desire to abandon Victorian standards and seek more equality with men.

Slimness not only was important because of fashion requirements but more significantly as a symbol of the New Woman. The plump Victorian matron and the ideals of self-sacrifice, nurturing and devotion to others were replaced with the ideal of the thin, contoured body — a symbol of freedom, power and control. Outward appearance took on an important role for women. The cultural prescription enforced the belief that the size and shape of the body was a measure of self-worth and that beauty was achievable through hard work. Controlled consumption was necessary to self-improvement and lack of control was seen as self-indulgence. (19)

The female body, because of its reproductive function, typically has a 25% fat content, while 15% is normal for males. From an evolutionary standpoint, millions of years ago when food resources were uncertain, the female body most likely developed its extra cushion of fat as a reserve supply of nutrition. A pregnancy requires 80,000 calories and body fat is utilized in the production of milk. Physicians agree that a certain level of fat is needed to maintain the cycle of ovulation. (20)

However, fleshiness is viewed with disgust and equated with nurturing, femininity, passivity — qualities that our American culture does not value. On the other hand, thin, muscularly toned bodies are perceived as symbols of strength, independence, control, power and success — values that our culture deifies.

Our obsession with thinness is reflected in the fact that the number of articles dealing with diets and dieting which appear annually in women's magazines doubled between 1959 and 1979. (21)

Dieting has become a consuming passion for some, a preoccupation for others. The esthetic ideal of beauty and femininity has had far-reaching consequences for young girls and women. A few years ago, dissatisfaction with the body generally became more pronounced when girls advanced into adolescence. The physiological reality is that before puberty, girls have 10-15 percent more body fat than boys — but after puberty, girls have almost twice as much fat as boys. (22) Physical maturation for girls moves them *away from* the cultural ideal of being thin whereas, for boys, the weight spurt is predominantly due to an increase in muscle and lean tissue. Physical maturation for boys moves them *toward* the masculine physical ideal.

Concerns over body shape and weight have an impact on pre-adolescents. A University of California study found that of 500 girls surveyed in grades 4 through 12, 31 percent of 9 year olds said they worry that they are fat or might become overweight. (22) Although 58 percent of the girls in the study said they considered themselves overweight, analysis of their height and weight showed only 17 percent really were!

Fifty-nine percent of teen-aged girls would like to lose weight while 52 percent of teen-aged boys think their weight is fine and 28 percent of *those* boys would like to *gain* weight. (22) A Gallup poll shows that about a third of women aged 19-39 diet at least once a month. (23) These results reflect that women and young girls have learned to fear fat and to view fleshiness as ugly and detestable.

In a survey conducted by a national magazine, three-quarters of the 9,000 women who responded said that shape and weight were the most important factors determining their feelings about their bodies. Twelve percent of the respondents said they were extremely dissatisfied with their bodies, 16 percent were quite dissatisfied and 25 percent were somewhat dissatisfied. What the women liked least and wanted most to change were their hips, thighs, buttocks, stomachs and waists — areas where, biologically, women are designed to carry more fatty tissue than men. (23) (24)

As we women have become intensely preoccupied with our weight and with controlling our appetites, a new mentality has emerged which is very dangerous to our psychological well-being.

We define our worth by our ability to restrain or control our appetites; we view ourselves as "good" if we abstain from certain foods which we view as "bad" such as sugar-laden sweets, breads, butter, etc. On the other hand, we see ourselves as bad when we give in to our desires and are unable to control eating those foods that have been designated as bad.

We then determine our self-worth whether we are good or bad, a success or a failure, by if and what we have eaten and by how much we weigh. Not only is self-definition rigidly connected to external appearance but we believe that if anything goes wrong with our lives — bad romance, no job promotion, etc. — it must be the fault of our bodies — *If only I were thinner, I would have been given that raise.*

Standards of beauty are often connected to broader political and economic issues. According to Freedman, "The lean image conforms to our American value system, which admires hard work and self-denial. Slimness takes on virtuous connotations that are linked with economic success while overweight is viewed as shameful and lower class. Today, fat is considered unsightly because it represents low social status as well as a lack of self-control." (25)

Obsession with dieting and thinness has been one of the major contributors to the increase in eating disorders in this country. Exercise has also become another vehicle to achieving the perfect body. Fitness centers are as prolific as fast food restaurants and just as busy. Men, but particularly women, are dancing and jumping frenetically to the beat of music and an instructor's breathy countdowns. For some, this experience can, in fact, be a positive step toward maintaining aerobic conditioning. For others, however, it may have long-lasting adverse physical consequences.

Sandy, a 38-year-old bulimic, sought treatment because she had developed serious knee and back problems as a result of her twice daily aerobics and running regimen. She was told by her physician to stop all exercise until her injuries had a chance to heal. She panicked and was deeply depressed by the time she contacted the treatment center.

"There is no way I can stop exercising," she sobbed at her initial interview. "I will get fat if I do. I have been running — but only for an hour instead of my usual two. I have totally stopped aerobics but I do ride a stationary bike for 45 minutes every day. My knees and back are getting worse. I'm at the point of taking muscle relaxers in order to exercise." Sandy's voice was filled with desperation and fear. When she was told we would have to contact her physician and that we would support her physician's recommendations while at the same time trying to help Sandy deal with her anxiety and fears, she just nodded her head and became very quiet. It was obvious that she was not going to stop her exercising even though it could very well mean permanent damage to her body. We never saw her again.

A great number of our patients who are bulimic turn to obsessive exercising as a way of offsetting their binge behavior/high caloric intake. Although these women are suffering from an addictive illness, they express — to an extreme degree — what most women feel about their bodies.

The exercise movement has been followed by a more desperate attempt to alter the body. If weight or flesh can't be sweated off by exercise or made over with make-up, then the recourse is the surgeon's knife. Outpatient cosmetic surgery centers are becoming as popular as video stores. Facelifts, rhinoplasty (nose jobs), tummy tucks, breast augmentation, breast reduction, liposuction (surgery to remove excess body fat) and buttocks lifts are the most recent ways for women and men to achieve the cultural ideal of beauty.

In 1949, 15,000 purely cosmetic operations were performed in the United States. (24) A survey conducted by the American Society of Plastic and Reconstructive Surgeons reported more than a half a million purely cosmetic operations in 1986, a 24 percent increase over 1984 alone. (24) Statistics also reveal that increasingly men are choosing to have cosmetic surgery. (24)

Surgery, frenetic aerobics, weight lifting, restrictive dieting — all are attempts to restructure, remold the human body so it will be beautiful, admired and eternally youthful. This narcissistic obsession keeps us focused on the image we must create to prove we are strong, independent and in control. It keeps us stuck in the collective shame because we continue to feel separated from God/Nature, from each other and from our inner selves, always reaching for the elusive prescribed ideal. (25)

The barbarism of dieting, frenetic exercising and surgery might perhaps not appear as cruel as foot binding. However, the pain is felt not only as masochistic self-denial, which manifests itself in gastric and bowel problems, irritability, lethargy, anxiety, fatigue, insomnia and depression but more significantly, it is experienced as a wrenching emptiness within. Marion Woodman (26) calls it the "presence of an absence," a simple definition of addiction, which is rooted in a pervasive sense of alienation.

In her book, *The Hunger Strike* (27), Susie Orbach says that a woman's sense of her own body is the result first of how she believes her body measures up to the cultural ideal and second of the feelings she has developed about her body from childhood on. If a woman has developed reasonably positive feelings about her body, body shape and bodily functions, she can withstand the pressures of a culture that fosters shame and insecurity in women. However, it is very difficult to ignore the billboards, the magazine covers and ads, the television commercials and the radio ads which intrude on our daily life.

For those of us who have grown up in a dysfunctional family system, we are more likely to be vulnerable to the media and fashion/cosmetics industries which promote the belief that we can feel happier inside and realize our dreams if only we looked ideal on the outside.

The rejection of the female body in its natural form, in its reflection of the power of nature, mirrors the cultural rejection of the feminine principle.

When fashion is a tyrant rather than an expression of art or elegance, when it is the arbiter which determines whether one is acceptable or not, it becomes one more means of shame formation. It is important to redefine what is beautiful; to move it from the outside to the inside. Beauty is health, it is vulnerability, it is the vitality that comes from a sense of wholeness and oneness.

Beauty is not confined to one sex or the other. Our challenge is to view beauty for what it is and not for what it can fill within us.

In 1982, *Time* magazine, defining "The New Ideal of Beauty," said, "Throughout history women have been alternately starved and stuffed, and no one can guarantee that next year's body heroine won't be Dolly Parton. [This article was written before Dolly lost a lot of weight.] But to imagine this is to ignore the strides the contemporary woman has taken in the past dozen years and the good sense she has shown in achieving her new status. Medicine has made her more aware of how her body works. The fitness phenomenon has proved she has the capacity to make it work. Her new sense of self-assurance has convinced her that strength — of the body, mind and will — is beautiful." (16) And where does her spirit, her inner self fit into this scheme of beauty?

Social Expectations For Men

For men, social expectations are not without pressure. However, they do not typically focus on appearance as much as they do on job, intelligence and power. In contrast to women, research indicates that men tend to be more satisfied with their bodies. Body dissatisfaction, for them, tends to be focused on being underweight. Traditional men's magazine ads promote increasing muscle mass. This body standard — bulging, tight, sinewy muscles, broad shoulders, small waist — does promote bodyshame in men. There is little research in this area; since the world of the inner feelings of men is such uncharted territory, the masculine stereotype of aggression, logic, decisiveness and rationality remains intact.

Based on our work with men, we have discovered that they do experience bodyshame which is tied to the male stereotype. They are in a real bind since stereotypically they are not supposed to experience feelings and especially not discuss them. Since they are supposed to be decisive and rational, being overweight is in direct contradiction to their masculinity. The overweight male feels great shame about his body but it is shame connected to fear of being exposed as feminine, that is, weak, emotional, out of control.

Men with eating disorders have the same bodyshame as women regarding bodily hunger, sex drive and the like.

Bodyshame

If we examine shame in terms of the dissatisfaction with their bodies that women experience, we can see how a major source of shame for women and men who do not meet the patriarchal standard of physical acceptability focuses on the body itself.

In earlier discussion, we examined two forms of shame: being ashamed in front of others and being ashamed in front of the self. We mentioned that two common factors of shame involve fear of exposure and defectiveness. Typically, we think of such exposure and defectiveness as an inner trait or quality that falls short of our ideal self-image.

Shame implies that the defect is inherent in our personhood, our character. Bodyshame moves the feeling to the outer, more exposed self, the shell or container of the defective inner self.

For men and women who do not meet the cultural expectation of what is physically acceptable, shame becomes a dual exposure. *Not only am I intrinsically defective because I cannot control my inner desires and appetites but I am also extrinsically defective because my body does not meet standards of acceptability which would and could hide my inner defectiveness.* This objectification of the body can lead to a chronic self-consciousness, a compulsive comparing with others, which contributes to deeply entrenched feelings of shame.

Angela, an attractive 31-year-old compulsive overeater who is overweight, constantly compared herself to others.

Given her terribly low self-esteem, she was very reluctant to enter our group program. After several months of individual therapy, she finally agreed to participate. At the end of the first session, she said, "I just don't know how these people can relate to me. There are women in there who are married to doctors, who have graduate degrees, who have gone to better schools than I. Some of them aren't nearly as fat as I am and they have nicer skin than I do. Whenever I feel that someone is better looking than I am or has a better body than I do or is more educated than I am, I experience a deep aching pain that I feel to the bottom of my very soul. That pain has a voice which chants the same phrase over and over again, *"Angela, you just don't have what it takes. You just aren't good enough."*

Her feelings of inferiority were constantly fueled by her obsessive need to compare herself with everyone. No matter who Angela met, she always found something about that person to make them better than she was. Her entire sense of identity was shame based. As a result, her world was limited — at the time of treatment, it consisted only of her immediate family. Once she made up her mind to enter treatment, she was eager to reshape her life but believed the only way that could happen was if she re-shaped her body. That would make her feel as though she did have control over her unhappiness which, by the way, was rooted in her inner emptiness.

In this chapter, we have discussed the role of the culture in the shaming of the feminine and the female body. We have discussed how our hierarchical system of social structure sets men and women up for what we term "the collective shame experience." The collective shame experience is the process of denying, rejecting and negating the feminine aspects of ourselves, which ultimately results in a sense of fragmentation, disconnection and alienation from God/Nature, from ourselves and from each other.

We have also discussed the history of the shaming of the female body. Our particular focus has been on the degree to which this shaming has been disguised as beautification through fashion, cosmetics, dieting and exercise, even reconstructive surgery.

Though the shaming of the female body has been primary to our culture for centuries, men are no longer immune to the social expectations of physical perfection which have become equated with inner strength.

In next chapter, we will move from the global shaming of the body to the more personal element of the development of individual body image. We will also explore how shaming occurs on a more individualized basis.

4

Shame And Body Image

Just as everyone has a self-image and a sense of self-esteem so, too, we have a body image. Simply defined, body image is the mental representation or internal picture we have of our physical body, an inner view of our outer selves.

Body image, like self-esteem, can be positive and accurate or it can be negative, critical and vague. While built on our physical characteristics, it can remain quite independent of the reality of these characteristics. Since it is a product of our imagination, body image can easily be distorted. In spite of its changeability, for body image may be in a state of frequent flux, it *feels* very real and can be a source of pride or a source of great pain and dissatisfaction. (1)

Body image is very vulnerable to outside feedback. A flirtatious whistle can make us smile with pride while a critical comment or judgmental facial expression about our weight or body size from a significant person can make us cringe in shame.

Body Image And Physical Development

Most of us do not have an accurate image of our body. This is due to the fact that we learn about our bodies in a haphazard manner, partly because of the nature of physiological development and partly because it is impossible to see all dimensions of our bodies without the aid of several mirrors. (2)

James O. Lugo and Gerald L. Hershey (3) in their text, *Human Development*, state, "The body is the single most significant avenue for expression of the child's total self . . . Children actually construct varying physical self-images depending on their stage of development. The total of these self-images includes both ideal images of what could be and realistic images based on past experiences. Together, these images make up an integrated physical self-concept, which is but one component of the total self-concept." (3)

Human beings and the human body are perpetually changing and growing in the physical, emotional and cognitive realms. These three realms are continuously interrelating and influencing each other. For the purposes of our discussion, we will focus first on the physical or biological developmental process.

Physical Development

"Mass activity" is typical of infancy. As the infant receives physical and emotional nurturance, this mass activity becomes more specific and is then integrated into the child's behaviors, interactions and concept of self and others.

Lugo and Hershey use the example of hunger. When an infant experiences hunger, her whole body seems to quiver with this experience. As she grows, she will develop more specific feelings and responses to her hunger. Instead of quivering all over, she may develop a special sound or reaching movement to communicate her need.

It is also believed that physical coordination and concept occurs from the head to the toes (the cephalocaudal sequence) and from the center of the body outward (proximal-distal sequence). Again, referring to Lugo and Hershey, "Examples of cephalocaudal development are that at birth 25 percent of the infant's focal control resides in his head movements and the first step toward walking begins in head and neck control. A proximal-distal sequence is seen in the development of reaching. At first, the major activity centers around the torso and shoulders and then gradually moves to the arms, hands, and fingers." (4)

The way we learn about our bodies depends on two general types of physical development: sensory and perceptual development and motor development.

Sensory And Perceptual Development And Motor Development

Sensory and perceptual development includes both the internal and the external realms. Lugo and Hershey state that there are three major ways an individual receives information regarding the body through inner and outer experiences. (3)

The first way is by proprioceptors. These are the senses of smell, taste and the cutaneous (skin) senses of touch, pressure, pain and sensitivity to temperature.

Another avenue of sensory and perceptual development involves interoceptors. These include the sense of active movement through the muscles, tendons and joints; receptors in the inner ear which provide information about the body's reference to space and receptors in the inner organs which provide information regarding bodily functions.

Motor development is the process of the development of physical movement and skills. As indicated earlier, this process through which learning and understanding of the human body takes place begins with gross or large muscle movement. As maturation occurs, the more refined or fine motor actions and skills develop. For example, a gross motor skill is walking; a fine motor skill is putting on shoes and socks.

Of course, sensory and perceptual development and motor development are influenced by neurological development — the growth of the nervous system whose organization controls the sending and receiving of messages throughout the entire body.

Generally, we can say that our concept of our body changes as our ability to sense, perceive and move matures. As human beings, we are not and cannot be born with a concept of our whole bodies. We learn about our bodies through its natural growth process and the experiences into which this process draws us to participate.

Activities which facilitate our body awareness include proper nutrition, interaction between child and others which involves cooperative and imitative movements and the encouragement of autonomous movement. These can be given by the caretaker by providing suitable space for the youngster to move around in; appropriate physical contact and play; toys and games to promote the development of various physical skills and competencies and encouragement, not force, from significant adults so the child can explore the environment and the body itself. (3)

Body Image And Self-Esteem

There is a relationship between body image and self-esteem, although the dynamics of the relationship vary from person to person. Research indicates that a high degree of satisfaction with one's body is strongly associated with a high self-concept. (1) Body image, body satisfaction and self-image are positively related. In one study, women who perceived themselves as thin had a better self-image than those who felt they were average weight. (2) Perception of body is an important factor in the perception that individuals have of themselves.

Many of our group members frequently report that when they were thinner, they liked themselves better, had more self-confidence and got along better with others. This, of course, is also part of the addictive cycle of dieting. The chronic dieter tries to recapture the feeling of success — *I am good when I am in control of my eating* — that she had when she was restricting her food intake and losing weight — *I look good when I am thinner.*

When she deviates from her diet regimen, however, she swings into a shame cycle in which she begins to hate herself — *I am bad because I am out of control* — and feels fat — *I look bad when I'm fat.* Her body image and self-image can dramatically change from acceptable to awful with just a few cookies. Consequently, shame may become a dominant theme in her body image and her self-image.

Body Image Disturbance

Body image disturbance is experienced by most women in Western culture and can be a serious problem. It occurs when an individual has distorted thoughts, feelings and perceptions with regard to her body; usually the individual's perception is different from her actual size, shape and appearance. Body image disturbance is a multifaceted phenomenon which includes the following issues: body size distortion, body size dissatisfaction, insensitivity to interoceptive cues and concern with body shape. (5)

Body image disturbance can also include distortions of certain body parts — thighs, arms, breasts, legs — which individuals see as fat, ugly, too big, too small, shriveled, etc. These defective body parts seem to dominate the entire physical self and influence the overall feelings these individuals have about themselves.

Miriam, a 32-year-old bulimic, entered our treatment program with a disparaging view of herself and her body. Though she was at an average weight for her height and bone structure, Miriam saw herself as fat. Her fat image focused on her hips, which she felt were much wider (and therefore fatter) than they should be. When other group members commented on her attractiveness, Miriam would look at them in shock and reply incredulously, "How can you say that? I'm so fat and I feel so big, especially in my hips." She pounded her hips with her fists as she spoke. "They are so big. You know, I can't stand to look at myself in the mirror when I'm undressed." As she averted her gaze from the group, tears spilled onto her lap.

Despite the fact that others objectively saw her as attractive, Miriam saw herself as defective and her body as proof of her inferiority. She was unable to move beyond what she perceived as defective and to focus on her personal and physical strengths.

Body image disturbance influences the individual's eating patterns and greatly affects self-esteem in a negative feedback loop. For example, a woman who feels fat may eat or binge in response to her anxiety about her body. This eating or binging behavior deepens her sense of failure thereby lowering her self-esteem.

Body image disturbance is one of the more common and accepted symptoms of anorexia, bulimia and compulsive eating. In our experience, we have noted that women of average weight and those who are slightly overweight tend to see themselves as bigger than they are, while our more overweight patients tend to see themselves as smaller than they are. Some of our obese patients report not having a sense of their bodies below the head and neck.

Influential Factors In Body Image Formation

There are several influential factors that affect a person's body image either positively or negatively.

Interactions And Attitudes Of Primary Caregivers

Much like psychological development, body image formation is highly influenced by the interactions and attitudes of the primary caregivers. However, adolescence is a particularly critical time for body image formation since this image is the one we typically carry throughout our adult lives.

Early Childhood Influences

In early childhood, body awareness and body image development is strongly influenced by the identification process (6) as well as by how significant adults deal with the child's feelings about her body (the interest in exploring it), the child's drive states and the child's needs as they relate to the body.

Prebirth Expectations

Ann Kearney-Cook, an expert in body image disturbances (7), states that body image development begins prior to birth. When a woman becomes pregnant, the couple has an image of the way they would like their baby to look. Their idealized image of this baby is influenced by their own body image history.

If the child's physical appearance is acceptable to the parents, then its emotional needs will be met within the context of an accepting and loving relational environment which contributes to the infant's feelings of self-worth — the basis for a healthy body image (8).

Body Awareness

The basic foundation of the psychological self is the awareness of the body. Body concept emerges from an awareness of internal and external kinesthetic sensations, somatic movements, mental representations and maturation. Body awareness is connected to the process of separation/individuation starting at approximately six months and continuing until individuation is achieved at about 23 months. At 1 to 14 months of age, as the infant's motor activity increases, the primary caretaker begins to identify the various body parts for the infant. In mirroring the infant's interest in its body, the mother assists the child in developing a body awareness. From 14 to 24 months the infant's body becomes more differentiated from the mother and it will actually resist being put in various positions. (9) As psychological separateness occurs so too does the body engage in more independent activity.

Psychological and physical development depend on the relationship that develops between mother and infant. Initially, the relationship between mother and infant is basically a tactile one involving feeding, changing, hugging, rocking, dressing, cooing and gazing.

The body reminds the infant of its vulnerability — the hunger pangs it feels when it has not been fed, the temperature fluctuations of heat or cold while not being able to remove or pull up its own blankets, the diaper pin that jabs its flesh and cannot be removed. All of these physical pains and sensations are a vivid reminder to the infant of its dependency upon the caretaker.

The mother is responsible for assisting the child in its physical development. The mother helps the child to sit or to stand, she holds her arms out to reach for the child, she offers praise and applause as the child accomplishes new physical tasks. The mother encourages exploratory and reaching behaviors. This interchange is essential to the child as it gains a greater awareness of its physical self and its increasing mobility.

The mother attempts to anticipate the child's need for sleep, for food or for attention. She dresses the child so that it will be comfortable. In all of these ways, the relationship between mother and child is the basis for the baby's capacity to understand its physical and psychological self.

Dysfunctional Families

The dysfunctional family is typically characterized as having boundary issues, communication problems, rigid rules, perfectionistic standards and difficulty with change or transition. These families have difficulty recognizing their children as separate individuals, as having a distinct body and a range of feelings. The children are perceived as an extension of the parents or of their feelings, bodily experience or desires. The parents are unable to let the child experience autonomous and internally directed actions.

The children's emotions and bodies are not seen by their parents as separate entities. The parents are incapable of effective mirroring, of affirming the child's uniqueness and psychic boundaries. Consequently they often do not experience the distinctness of their body boundaries. These individuals do not have a coherent, cohesive, organized body image. For them, there has been a failure in the early months of life to acknowledge and arrive at a body self that is separate from the caregiver.

They are estranged from their bodies. They do not have a sense of internal bodily sensations, so they starve or binge in order to feel something inside. They do not have a sense of external bodily sensations, so they exercise frenetically or wear clothing that will stimulate their skin — anything to help them *feel*.

Heidi, a 39-year-old compulsive eater and exerciser who entered treatment saying she felt "nothing, inside or out," recalls that her mother always answered for her. In one of their family therapy sessions when Heidi was 16 years old, she recalls that the therapist asked Heidi when she first started to binge. "My mother didn't miss a beat and responded, 'We didn't start binging until last year.' I remember feeling such rage! But all I did was nod my head in agreement. The therapist asked me how I felt about my body. My mother replied, 'Oh, we don't really like our hips. We have the same hips. They really are big.' "

In these families, the children are used as objects to verify the success of the family. Problems occur if any of the children are less than perfect. These parents, as a result of their own low self-esteem and early birth family dysfunction, look to their children as image makers.

When Ashley was a teenager, she had tremendous weight fluctuations. In a fat period, she recalls, "It was my parents' 25th anniversary and they were having a huge party. They invited relatives and friends from all over the country. A few weeks before the party, my mom and I went shopping for a dress for me. Nothing fit well and every time I tried on another dress, my mother would just heave a deep sigh of despair. She looked as though she were just disgusted with me.

"Finally, I said to her, 'Maybe I shouldn't go to the party. You could just tell everyone I was sick.' Suddenly, my mother's face lit up and, to my great shock, she said, 'That's a wonderful idea! Then you won't embarrass your father and me.' "

As she describes this scene, Ashley stares into space, far removed from her feelings, and says, "I just can't believe that she didn't want me there."

These children have a difficult time proving their sense of individuality and often their one area of control revolves around food and weight.

As we have discussed, the mutual responsiveness that infants and children need to develop a positive self-image and body image is both emotional and physical in nature. If the child's actual appearance measures up to the parents' ideal image, the parents will have a more accepting attitude toward the child and consequently will be more responsive emotionally and physically. This attitude will be reflected in the way the parents hold the child, the kind of touch felt by the child and the way the parents talk to and about the child.

In a dysfunctional family, the child may experience rejection from the parents if she does not measure up to the idealized image that the parents have or does not have positively valued family characteristics or has marked birth defects. This rejection occurs because the family is fearful of exposing its shame and may see the child's "defect" as putting the family at higher risk for exposure as a failure.

One of our primary ways of expressing rejection is through withdrawal. This withdrawal is generally both emotional and physical. It is easy to see how a young child may construe a caretaker's inability to respond to its needs or avoidance of physical and emotional contact as rejection and this can be the basis for the development of bodyshame and selfshame in the growing child.

Parents' Attitude About The Body

Another factor that can cause bodyshame in the developing child is the parents' level of acceptance or shame regarding the human body generally and his or her own body image specifically. We have discussed how this shaming of the human body makes the desire to explore, understand and experience pleasure through the body an evil, repulsive act. Yet all children are naturally curious and the desire to explore and experience pleasure through the body is part of learning and developing a solid body image.

The caretaker's response to this curiosity will strongly influence the child's later feelings about the body. If the child explores her body and finds delight in the experience, the mother who has her own bodyshame may grab the child's hand and slap it, letting the youngster know that the body is not only something you don't touch but, more important, something you don't get pleasure from. This is a particular problem for mothers and their daughters, given our cultural expectations.

Identification And Gender Expectations

Because of the social ramifications of gender, mothers and daughters have a particularly complicated relationship which can greatly affect the development of bodyshame and selfshame in the daugther.

In mothering a girl, the mother is raising her daughter to be like her. In mothering a boy, the mother is raising him to be an "other." Due to the socialization differences of gender, mothers relate very differently to their female children than to their male children. Much of the difference is intentional and adheres to the sex role stereotyping required by our culture. Other differences are very subtle and promoted through the mother's unconscious feelings about what is feminine and what is masculine.

The feelings a woman has about her femininity are an essential part of what she brings to her role as a mother. When a mother looks at her daughter, she often identifies with her, based on their shared gender identity, social roles and social expectations. She transmits the process of her own physical and psychological feminine experience.

Consequently, she may pass along the negative feelings about her own feminine side.

When a mother looks at a son, she sees someone who is different. This difference in gender helps the mother to be more cognizant of her boundaries. Not so with a daughter. Boundaries with a daughter, are easily blurred.

Femininity, Beauty And Thinness

Being female is associated with beauty and softness from the earliest days of a child's life and being male is associated with aggressiveness and toughness. (10)

Research in early childhood development demonstrates that parents of girls described their infant daughters as beautiful, soft, pretty, cute and delicate while they rated their sons as strong, larger featured, better coordinated and hardier. (11) In another study, when asked what kind of person they wanted their children to become, parents mentioned being attractive and having a good marriage far more often for daughters than for sons. (12)

Parents felt that one of a little girl's major jobs is to look pretty. Little girls learn very early that being attractive is connected with pleasing and serving others, which will, in turn, secure love and acceptance. Research indicates that mothers treat their infant daughters with more caution and fear, curtailing their exploratory behaviors when it exceeds a certain physical distance from the mother. However, when it comes to sons, mothers are more apt to let boys explore the environment and will allow for a greater physical distance. (13)

Mother's Influence

A little girl looks to her mother in admiration when she dresses up in high heels, fusses with make-up, jewelry, etc. She gazes in utter amazement at the transformation of her mom. She sits for what seems like hours as her mother pokes at her eyes, pats her face, picks at her eyebrows and rouges her cheeks.

When mommy complains about her weight or shrieks as she gets on the scale, the little girl learns quite emphatically that the female body is not acceptable as it is.

At mealtimes, the little girl observes her mother weighing food or sometimes not eating at all. She hears her recite a litany of calories for each item on the table. These memories will permeate her idea of what it means to be a *girl*.

The mother transmits the cultural definition of femininity to her daughter in some very direct and some very subtle ways. Through identifying with a mother whom the child perceives as powerless and dissatisfied with her body, the child may grow up disliking her own body. Daughters often associate the bodily flaws of their mothers as evidence of inferiority and assume they are the basis for the mother's discontent and unhappiness.

Since mothers were little girls once too, they have their own feelings about their bodies, influenced by their own mothers. The mother is the major force in shaping the daughter's feelings about her body and her sexuality.

In dealing with her daughter's body, the mother has to teach a daughter how to deal with the many changes her body will undergo in her lifetime. These changes are not only related to menstruation and breast development but also to fluctuating body weight. A woman's body image changes constantly since her weight fluctuates in tandem with her menstrual/ovulation cycle. Some days she feels *fat*, while on other days she feels *normal*. These bodily changes have a direct impact on her self-image. As a role model, the way that the mother deals with her own bodily changes has a critical impact on the daughter's body image.

Girls experience shame as their interest and curiosity is met with contempt, fear or anger. Whether it's environmental exploration or bodily exploration, the little girl learns that this feeling of interest and initiative is shameful. As a result, females feel cautious about their need to initiate, to explore, to go beyond. They look to others for approval and validation and only when they receive it do they feel free to move.

Through parental feedback, verbal and nonverbal, children learn that a boy's body is to be strengthened and actively developed through athletic activities whereas a girl's body is to be protected and made attractive.

Marlene, a 43-year-old compulsive eater, was the only girl in a family of four. She remembers clearly that Saturdays were the worst day of the week for her. Every Saturday morning her brothers would go out and shoot baskets. She desperately wanted to go out and play with them. However, her mother continually reprimanded her for wanting to play with the boys. She was likely to get hurt and be "scarred for life," her mother said. "Who would want to marry you if you were scarred or deformed? Look at me, your father left me 'cause I'm big and fat. That's how men are. If you're not perfect, they don't want you." She could never understand why Marlene didn't want to stay home with her and clean house (including her brothers' bedrooms). Her reward for helping her mother houseclean was to go shopping, when they would spend time perusing the clothing departments and make-up counters.

Adolescence

The physical changes that occur in adolescence do not take place in a linear fashion. They interact within the context and culture of a society. The adolescent growth spurt, the body shape and weight changes, the onset of sexual maturation and hormonal fluctuations have a tremendous impact on the adolescent's personality and behavior. Concurrently, the attitudes and values acquired from the culture and the family have an effect on the adolescent's reaction to bodily changes. Developing a comfortable body image is a major task of adolescence.

Even more difficult for the adolescent to cope with is that these physical changes are not a uniform process. There is an unevenness in the growth rates of the adolescent's various body parts and functions which can make the young person feel awkward and self-conscious.

Preoccupied with their looks and appearance, adolescents are painfully sensitive to any physical differences they may have from their peer group. Consequently they may have a difficult time coping with the sudden and intense physical changes that take place both inside and outside their bodies.

Coming to terms with the critical adolescent question, *Who Am I?* means forming a new body image and integrating the new physical self into one's self-concept. This integration is critical since the body image formed in adolescence is the one we carry throughout our adult lives.

Due to the many bodily changes of puberty, adolescence is an extremely fertile time for the emergence and formation of bodyshame. Several factors contribute to the development of bodyshame at this critical stage of human development.

Factor One: Parental Attitude
Toward The Changing Body

As we have indicated, dysfunctional families are characterized by their lack of communication, inability to deal with feelings and with overinvolvement or underinvolvement among family members. They also have difficulty with changes and transitions. The bodily changes of the adolescent signal a major developmental change for the family as a whole, particularly for the parents.

If it is difficult for the parents to accept their own bodies or natural bodily functions, it will be particularly tough to understand and be supportive of the adolescent's ever mercurial feelings about bodily changes.

If a daughter is prematurely developing secondary sexual characteristics (pelvic bone enlargement, fat deposits in the pelvic area, breast development), mother may react with anxiety, wondering if her daughter will be ridiculed. Dad may suddenly withdraw his attention and physical touching of his daughter, uncertain how to deal with her emerging womanhood. This is particularly true for dads who have distorted views of femininity and female sexuality.

Mother may feel uncomfortable with her son's changing body, testicular and penile growth and his first ejaculation or wet dreams. Dad may be concerned about his son's sexual adequacy and fear his son's sexual curiosity.

Changing bodies and raging hormones signal the emerging sexual needs and drives of the adolescent. Parents become frightened about bodily changes and equate them with sexual activity. They do not view the sexual activity of their daughters in the same light as that of their sons. Although the women's movement has done much to equalize and recognize women's sexual drives and needs as healthy and normal, there is still a tendency to treat the adolescent female's emerging sexuality with more caution and fear. The threat of pregnancy often contributes to the parents' anxiety — another shame bind for the adolescent female.

How sympathetic is the parent to the child's bodily changes? The manner in which the onset of menarche is dealt with has an impact on a young girl's feelings about this bodily function. A sudden growth spurt for a young boy coupled with an ever changing and cracking voice needs support and understanding from parents and siblings rather than ridicule and teasing. These bodily changes can precipitate a shame response if parents and siblings ridicule or exhibit a sense of shame over developing sexuality.

Bodily changes also signal emerging independence and autonomy. The ability of mothers and fathers to respond to their sons' and daughters' bodily and emotional changes at adolescence is a chief contributor in the development of selfshame and bodyshame. If mother and dad share joy in their child's emerging self, embrace the natural alterations arising in the parent-child relationship — the affectional bond moving toward the adult-to-adult level of mutuality versus the caregiver-care receiver level of interaction — then the child will experience herself as affirmed both physically and emotionally and will integrate a healthy self-image and body image.

Factor Two: Culturally Determined Standards
Of Physical Acceptability

Before we examine this factor more closely, we must remember that adolescent development poses a particular dilemma for girls.

As mentioned earlier, before puberty, girls have 10-15 percent more body fat than boys but, after puberty, girls have almost twice as much fat as boys. Boys' weight spurt is due to an increase in muscle and lean tissue. Given the cultural expectations for females to be thin — and for males to be muscular — it is no wonder that girls express lower body esteem than adolescent boys. (14) Their bodily changes move them away from the cultural ideal while bodily changes for boys move them much closer to what's acceptable.

According to the research (15), adolescent girls are very concerned with their looks and are aware of the great value that society places on physical attractiveness for women. Girls listed weight as their leading concern about their appearance.

Falling short of the cultural ideal generates shame for the adolescent female. Resolving the conflict between one's real and ideal body image is another nearly impossible task of adolescence. In comparing herself to the ideal, the adolescent girl will always fall short, particularly the adolescent who is unable to see her body realistically (disturbed body image).

Research (16) has demonstrated that the feedback boys receive from their teachers centers around their intellectual achievements whereas girls were more often praised for things unrelated to intellectual achievement, such as neatness, good grooming, etc.

The importance of appearance to girls is also promoted through the mass media and children's books. *Women on Words and Images* (14) revealed that the girls in these primers focused their attention on their looks whereas boys never did. Attending to one's appearance was a major activity for the female characters whereas male characters were more likely to be playing hard or solving problems. Television also promotes the cultural ideal of femininity and girls tend to internalize these standards. Developmental studies reveal that girls are more concerned than boys about their physical attractiveness. (14)

Even though menstruation and ovulation play a key role in the physiological functions of the female, the secondary sex characteristics play a greater social role in the way in which peers interact with adolescent girls. Breast, hip and thigh size can be a major source of shame or pride for girls. For adolescent boys, shame can result from a high-pitched cracking voice or a sudden erection. Shameful events, however, are more closely related to the shame of bodily functions than to the shame of falling short of the ideal and of what's considered beautiful and acceptable.

An additional complication in physical and psychological maturation for girls revolves around the notion that the self-image of a girl is more interpersonally oriented than a boy's. (17) Girls seem to worry more about what other people think of them, are more concerned about being liked and try harder to avoid negative reactions from others. (18) Girls are focused more on affiliation and interpersonal relationships. (19) They are concerned about being accepted by others whereas boys' adolescent issues seem to center on achievement, autonomy and control. Consequently, the adolescent girl becomes particularly sensitive to and compliant with social demands and appropriate sex role standards. This can exacerbate her shame feelings about her bodily fat and her need to control her body and appetites so that she can be better liked and valued.

Another shame-related bind that the adolescent girl becomes vulnerable to is her relational orientation. Gilligan (20) reported that adolescent girls conceptualize dependence as a positive attribute, with isolation as its polar opposite. This creates confusion and self-doubt in a culture that highly values independence and individualism and devalues dependence, viewing the latter as a serious flaw.

In gravitating toward others, the young girl tends to deny, ignore or suppress many of her needs and initiatives.

Young girls learn that their ability to form relationships, especially with males, often depends on the acceptability of their bodies.

The young girl begins to feel a sense of shame over her need for others, sadness when a relationship is somehow in turmoil, anxiety when there is conflict in a relationship. She is taught that these feelings are a form of weakness rather than learning to appreciate them as part of her unique female psychological development.

Research indicates (21) that when other aspects of life seem out of control, weight and eating may be the one area where the female adolescent can feel some self-control, some sense of strength and power. Weight and dieting can be tied to the adolescent's struggle for what the culture defines as independence. Dieting may reflect a girl's desire to show others as well as herself that she is growing up and independent. (22) This is something that she does not innately feel. She resists her relational needs and views them as bad.

Losing weight may symbolize an attempt to defy her body's changes and help her maintain a more childlike body, keeping her feeling safe in her dependency needs.

The culture in which an individual takes pride in being independent, in control, thin and powerful, also creates a shame-laden spirit for the emerging female who needs and values relationships and whose body fails to conform to the culture's body ideal.

Factor Three: Attitudes Of The Peer Group

The peer group assumes the central role in the life of the adolescent. The family is replaced. The peer group serves as a buffer between the family and the wider community that is not yet ready to accept the adolescent. (23)

The peer group holds up standards regarding attitudes toward authority figures, dress codes, sexual mores, social and academic performance, drug and alcohol use and appearance.

All of the research indicates that there is a correlation between physical attractiveness and popularity among adolescent peer groups. (16) This makes the need to be thin even more of a consuming passion for the female adolescent.

If the peer group centers around an activity which requires a certain weight or body type such as dancing, diving, swimming, wrestling or modeling then the adolescent will feel additional pressure to maintain a certain body type and weight.

Terri, an 18-year-old bulimic, had been a diver since she was seven years old. She showed great promise and her parents were extremely proud of her many diving accomplishments. At 13, however, her body started to change. Her coach began to pressure her about her weight. Terri wasn't the only one on the team, though, with a changing and growing body. She struggled with her diet and tried to maintain her weight. One day a group of her teammates asked her to go along with them for a pizza. She was surprised. "Well," she said, "I'd rather go somewhere else because I don't think I can withstand the temptation to eat pizza. Anyway, we have weigh-ins tomorrow." They all giggled and told her not to worry about the weigh-in. A teammate assured her she could eat pizza as much as she wanted and still make weight. "How can I do that?" Terri asked with great curiosity. Her teammate said, "You can eat as much pizza as you want and then you can vomit or take laxatives. We've been doing it for weeks now and it works! We can have our cake and eat it too!" When she hesitated, they continued to assure her that this was a great way to eat whatever she wanted and still maintain her diving weight. She finally agreed to go. They had frequent binge/vomit parties throughout high school. Her bulimia increasingly became a problem. Finally out of control, she sought treatment.

An individual's body changes constantly throughout life. However, these changes are not immediately incorporated into the body image. Research has demonstrated that a time lag exists between the actual body change and its integration into the person's body image. (2) This explains why an overweight person, who loses a great deal of weight, still sees herself as fat.

Ideals And Expectations Of The Culture

A person's self-esteem is partly her assessment of herself against an ideal model. In earliest life, this model is typically a parent or significant adult — even a media star. As we mature, our ideal self image becomes less dependent upon a specific model and more on an image of the way we would like to be. This image is a synthesis of the individuals we admired in the earlier stages of our development.

As we have discussed, shame theorists postulate that shame can be generated when the individual falls short of her idealized version of herself. The ideal versus the real image goes beyond the inner self and includes the body. Consequently, our ideal self image includes a mental representation of the body type we wish for.

The cultural standards promote a woman's tendency to have an idealized body image based on these standards. Whenever a woman becomes acutely aware that her real body falls far short of her ideal, she may experience deep feelings of shame. Many of our patients cite painful body-shame experiences.

Alyssa, who weighed 375 pounds, did not see herself as that large. When she arrived at a party, she tried to sit down in an armchair and was shocked to discover that she did not fit in it. The hostess, noticing that she might even break the chair since it was made of wicker, ran to Alyssa and quickly escorted her to another chair. Alyssa reported feeling a deep sense of shame as other guests saw what was happening. She was so ashamed that she left the party early, feigning illness. When she shared this experience in group, she sobbed uncontrollably, castigating herself for not realizing she was so large.

Faye, a bulimic whose real body size was about a size 10, had been rigidly dieting for several weeks. She felt certain that she had lost a lot of weight because her clothes were feeling quite loose. Since her closet contained what she called "fat clothes" and "thin clothes," she grabbed a pair of her thin jeans to change into at her boyfriend's apartment. When she got there, she began to change and as she was putting on her jeans, which refused to zip up, her boyfriend walked into the bedroom. When she caught his gaze, she reported feeling a profound sense of shame about her body. "I couldn't believe it," she sobbed. "He must think I'm a fat slob!"

Bodyshame is experienced not only in relation to falling short of the ideal but it is exacerbated by the shame-drive bind of hunger. The body is a visible source of shame that reveals a failure to keep our appetites in check. For women, the appetite encompasses more than just a hunger for food. It represents our inability to control our emotions and needs. We have examined this earlier.

The feelings of bodyshame are often related to early childhood and adolescent experiences which focused on the body or specific body parts. Once again, research strongly supports the notion that the body image formed in adolescence may be a major component of the adult's body image. (24)

Physical Trauma And Physical Boundary Violations

Body image can be deeply affected by traumatic experiences such as sexual abuse, surgery and physical deformity. Ann Kearney-Cook (24) postulates that a disturbance in body image could result from a sexual victimization experience, since the body is where the original trauma took place. The shameful feelings do not subside once the abuse ends.

Problems that survivors of sexual abuse may experience with their bodies include splitting, numbing, addictions and self-mutilation. (25) Initially, these are defenses developed by the sexual abuse survivor to cope and survive psychologically and emotionally. Because it was the body that was abused, survivors tend to blame their bodies. If this blaming (and shaming) continues, however, it will be hard for the survivor to heal from the sexual abuse and she may be further hurt emotionally, psychologically and physically by a defense system which is no longer useful. One of the defenses that a sexual abuse survivor may use is compulsive eating behavior. The specific reasons to use food compulsively may vary but initially it is for protection. Some sexual abuse survivors compulsively overeat, undereat or binge and purge as a sedative — a way to numb feelings of anger, hurt and shame. For others, eating compulsively is a way to be nurtured because the sexual abuse has either kept them from learning or too fearful to engage in any other forms of nurturance.

Some women who are survivors of sexual abuse will compulsively overeat and become overweight as a way to try to protect themselves physically. They hope that by being "big" and by not fitting into the cultural ideal of beautiful, no sexual attraction and consequently no sexual assault can occur. Conversely, the anorexic hopes that by starving she can keep her body from developing or showing any physical characteristics — for example, breasts — which would be seen as sexual and therefore risk promoting sexual contact.

Compulsive overeating which results in overweight, anorexia and bulimia are all efforts by the sexual abuse survivor to control her body and, in effect, try to get back the power she felt robbed of by the sexual abuse. It is important to note that individuals who have been physically and emotionally abused in ways other than sexual ones will experience the same sense of violation, shame and need for protection as the sexual abuse survivor. It is also important to note that sexual abuse is not confined to rape and incest. Sexual abuse includes any physical or emotional violation which takes place through coercion and intimidation. Women who have been the objects of inappropriate sexual kissing, caressing, staring, grabbing or conversation have experienced a form of sexual abuse and will often respond emotionally and physically just like the survivor of incest or childhood beatings.

Physical Disability And Deformity Trauma

Due to our society's emphasis on physical perfection and bodily control, individuals who are physically disabled or physically deformed through injury, illness or heredity quickly become aware that they are looked upon by others as inadequate and consequently inferior. The body image and self-concept of the individual who is physically different because of a deformity or disability is deeply affected by the attitudes and interactions of others and by what she is encouraged to learn and do.

Involvement in physical activity such as wheelchair sports is important to help the individual realize that she is more physically capable than she, and possibly others, have realized. Those with neurological disorders such as cerebral palsy need to become acquainted with their bodies through visual stimulation — looking at pictures, examination and conscious movement of the body and body parts. Beyond physical therapy, occupational therapy and psychotherapy, dance therapy is often used to allow these people to identify, explore and express feelings of anger, love, grief and guilt. It is useful in increasing body awareness and promotes mind/body integration.

As with physical, emotional and sexual abuse survivors, the individual trying to cope with a physical deformity or disability may use eating as a way to numb the hurt, the anger and the sense of isolation or to provide herself with nurturance. This is particularly needed because many people fail to or avoid making any physical contact with someone who has a physical deformity or disability.

A woman who has had a mastectomy may be angry with her body for "betraying" her as she tries to cope with the feelings of now, somehow, being "less of a woman." She is questioning her general physical and sexual attractiveness. Children with developmental disabilities which retard the development of motor skills or general physical signs of maturation may become frustrated with themselves and with their bodies for being different in an alienating way. Burn victims and other individuals with distinctly visible deformities are frequently stared at and experience a shame response in the wake of a sense of exposure and fear of judgment by others. (26)

Natural Process And Body Image Formation

Though essentially all of the human body's growth has occurred by early adulthood, the body continues to function and to change throughout adult life. Due to their reproductive powers and the culture's emphasis on beauty, women have a body image that is more subject to change.

Pregnancy

When a woman becomes pregnant, her body begins immediately to make the changes necessary to sustain the life and growth of the fetus and to prepare for childbirth. Until birth, the woman's body carries the fetus and all its vital life functions, as well as her own.

She will notice changes in energy level, hunger and her bowel and bladder functions as the fetus grows. Breasts grow larger in anticipation of lactation. Some women develop varicose veins, stretch marks across the abdomen and breasts and many experience puffiness with water retention in the joints. (27)

The pregnant woman has another life moving inside her that she cannot control. Again, due to our society's emphasis on thinness and appearances, many women suffer through pregnancy feeling fat and unattractive. Weight becomes a primary issue for both expectant mother and physician — though frequently for very different reasons.

Even though, with proper nutrition, moderate exercise and time, the woman's body will gradually return to its preconception state or close to it, many women, out of fear of being fat, will begin rigid diet and exercise routines immediately after birth to get their bodies back into shape. Others, who feel helpless and overwhelmed by the loss of bodily control through pregnancy, may continue this stance and do not properly take care of themselves physically or emotionally. They become overweight and physically inactive.

Menopause

Menopause is considered by some to be the only adult physiological change that resembles early childhood growth and the growth changes of puberty. Menopause is experienced differently both emotionally and physically by each woman.

For some, it occurs gradually; for others menopause arrives rather abruptly. Estrogen and progesterone hormone levels diminish and the ovaries stop producing eggs. The postmenopausal woman can no longer procreate.

Typical symptoms associated with menopause include hot flashes, irritability, mood swings and, sometimes, depression. Again, as with puberty and pregnancy, the woman feels and, to some extent is, out of control over her body. Many women, due to lack of knowledge regarding what their body is going through, become fearful of or angry with their bodies. Some women reportedly worry about losing their sexuality or femininity. For the vast majority of women, however, fears regarding aging are profoundly triggered by the onset of menopause. (27)

Aging

Like any other human developmental process, aging encompasses biological, cognitive, emotional and social realms. In our culture, aging women are particularly vulnerable to the development of body image disturbance as the process of aging removes them from the cultural ideal of what is considered attractive, sexual and acceptable.

Women frequently attempt to control the aging process through cosmetics, cosmetic surgery and rigid dieting and exercise. Though proper nutrition, moderate exercise and proper care of the skin, hair, etc. can promote attractiveness in the aging woman through increased vitality and enhanced self-esteem, they cannot stop aging. Consequently, many women become angry with and ashamed of their bodies and themselves because of this loss of control.

Pride/Shame Cycle

Body image, our inner view of our outer selves, is a critical factor in our overall definition of ourselves. It is highly influenced by early physical and emotional interactions with our parents, by cultural standards of beauty and by feedback from others.

There is a relationship between body image and self-image. Women who like their bodies generally like themselves, while the converse is also true.

Although most women in our Western culture do not have an accurate body image, individuals who have eating disorders have a more disturbed view of their bodies. As a result of their belief that thinness symbolizes power, independence and control and that fatness symbolizes weakness, dependence and lack of control, they fall victim to an addictive pride/shame cycle which deeply affects both their body image and self-image. The effect of this cycle is to divide the unity of the body and the self, changing a working partnership into outright warfare.

For individuals with eating disorders, the body becomes an object to be transformed, a tool or an instrument to be used to shore up one's faltering self-esteem. The body becomes the coverup for our inner nakedness. This obsession with size and shape and weight allows us to ignore what our bodies are really feeling.

The pride/shame cycle mirrors the diet/binge syndrome where achieving thinness (dieting) is worthy of pride and being fat (binging) is shameful. This cyclical relationship is a metaphor of our culture's preoccupation with control and perfectionism (the masculine principle).

In this chapter, we have explored the relationship between shame and body image. Our body image is the mental picture we have of what our bodies look like.

Most of us do not have an entirely accurate body image, in part because we develop our body image over an extended period of time. Factors which influence the development of our body image are physical and emotional in nature. At the physical level, these factors relate to sensory, perceptual and motor development. Emotionally, our body image formation is strongly influenced by such factors as our parents' expectations, attitudes and interactions. These focus primarily on their ability to encourage us as children to learn about and understand our bodies and their ability to encourage movement and exploratory activities such as reaching, running and climbing. Also, our parents' comfort with their own bodies and their ability to accept the changes which occur in our changing and developing bodies, particularly during our adolescence, have an extensive impact on our ability to adjust to our maturing physical selves in a healthy fashion.

Body image disturbance is not uncommon. However, it is most acute for individuals who have eating disorders.

Shame-based or dysfunctional families are major contributors to body image disturbance in young members. Shame about the body and the consequent development of body image disturbance is induced in these disruptive family systems by blurred boundaries, by treating the child, and therefore the child's body, as a symbol of family success or failure and by the parents' own selfshame and bodyshame issues.

Adolescence is a particularly vulnerable time in the formation of body image. Now, not only parents and family but peers and cultural attitudes and expectations have a greater impact.

Other factors which influence body image development and often produce bodyshame and body image disturbance include physical trauma and physical boundary violations and physical disability or deformity. For women, especially, even the natural processes of pregnancy, menopause and aging can provoke shame responses.

All these factors have one thing in common: idealization. Families, peers and the culture in general have an ideal body image that they compare themselves and everyone else to. This ideal body is our symbol of perfection — of being strong, independent, successful and, therefore, acceptable.

Our ability to learn through and embrace our body as a part of our being is diminished and we become highly susceptible to viewing our body as an object, as separate from ourselves. As objects, these bodies are to be controlled and they become symbols of success or failure, sources of pride or shame.

In the next chapter, we will share with you the personal stories of individuals with eating disorders who have committed themselves to a program of recovery. As part of this commitment, each has devoted time to exploring selfshame and bodyshame, how they evolved and continue to influence their lives.

5

Selfshame/Bodyshame Themes For The Compulsive Eater

While patients are in treatment, they are introduced to the concepts of bodyshame and self-shame as causal factors in the disease of compulsive eating. This is accomplished through bibliotherapy, writing assignments, intensive group therapy and body image sessions. The reading, writing and group experience focuses on the shame that has been perpetuated in the patients' family systems and how it became a part of their shame-based identity. Body image sessions use guided imagery as a way to assist patients to become aware of the shameful attitudes they have internalized regarding their inner selves and their bodies.

Shame Workshops are conducted periodically for individuals who are graduates of the treatment program. These workshops focus on the use of art and group discussion to help individuals to better understand their shame experience and how it may act as a barrier in the ongoing process of recovery.

These intensive groups and workshops have provided us with a wealth of information about the seeds of the self-shame and bodyshame experienced by compulsive eaters.

The primary selfshame or inner self themes that patients most frequently identify are: shame over a sense of perceived weakness, at not being always in control and at needing others; shame regarding the individual's emotional life and shame at not being perfect.

The primary bodyshame themes focused on the following body parts: the abdomen, thighs, upper arms, breasts, waist, buttocks.

In both sets of shame themes, we are seeing evidence of the shaming of the feminine. The selfshame experienced by our patients is related to their tendency to compare their inner selves to the culturally elevated, more valued masculine traits, of being strong, rational and able to handle anything. The bodyshame themes focus on those areas in which a female is naturally more corpulent.

Though perhaps many individuals might say they are ashamed of the same aspects of the inner self and of the body, the difference between individuals and the compulsive eater is the intensity of the shame experience.

While an individual who does not have an eating disorder or other addictive illness might be embarrassed about a public display of tears and try to hide his "emotional weakness," he is also likely to forgive himself for this. Not compelled to chastise himself unmercifully or to set up for himself an intricate, perfectionistic code of behavior, he can let go of the incident and get on with his life.

A woman may not like her body when it does not measure up to the current ideal of slenderness. She may diet, buy expensive cosmetics and develop an exercise program. But the difference between this woman and a woman with an eating disorder is the intensity of anger and contempt felt for the body. The compulsive eater sees her body's inability to reach the ideal as a visual indicator of her internal weakness and inferiority. She seeks either to escape or remold her body in order to hide her shame about the substandard person she perceives herself to be.

Idealization is the key factor here. Most people have ideals, standards they use as guideposts in setting goals or making life decisions. The person with an eating disorder, however, does not perceive the ideal as a guideline but rather as *the* goal. Whereas the person who is not suffering from the all-or-nothing thinking of addictive illness may strive to be assertive and may be upset with herself when she has an incident of nonassertive behavior, the woman with an eating disorder will see the nonassertive event as *proof* of her inherent weakness.

Because she has failed to reach and sustain the goal without any wavering, she feels she is nothing. The person with an eating disorder focuses her attention, energy and self-evaluation on the outcome of her efforts. The concept of process, the importance and value of the steps necessary to attain a goal and the notion that real learning occurs through taking the steps, not only through the event itself, is foreign. It is often inconceivable to the compulsive eater that life is a process, not simply a series of events.

When an individual perceives her real self as nothing, loneliness and a great fear of abandonment prevail. The basic human need to be connected and affiliated with others is severely threatened. This creates an obsession with being substandard as well as with idealization. The person with an eating disorder thinks she can only mend the breach between her substandard self and the rest of the world if she molds herself into the image of what is idealized.

This belief crystallizes itself into a framework of living which attempts *always* to be strong, rational, logical, in control, happy and calm; *never* to be needy, indecisive, unhappy, angry or otherwise emotional. The body is then a symbol of this idealization which, if it measures up to the current ideal, will get approval, love, acceptance and success for her. Striving for the ideal body is an attempt by the shame-based person with an eating disorder to make up for being less than perfect on the inside; it is an attempt to bridge the gap that she feels between herself and others caused by her inferiority.

When our patients shared the history of their shame, their early childhood shame themes generally centered around mistakes they made, not understanding a situation they felt they should have understood or were told they should have understood or being ridiculed by peers or family. At puberty and adolescence, shame focuses more on teasing regarding bodily changes, on making mistakes and on not knowing what to do in social situations. In these citings of shame themes we see the beginning and self-feeding of perfectionism (fear of making mistakes, expecting to know all things at all times, expecting to always know the right thing to do) and disruption in the interpersonal bridge (feeling ridiculed by peers or parents or suffering the disapproval or withdrawal of significant others caused by not living up to their expectations or standards). An ever deepening tunnel of shame, sadness and loneliness is created which the compulsive eater desperately tries to get out of but with limited success because the efforts to break free are based on a tenacious drive toward perfectionism.

Many people with eating disorders will talk about shame around their sexuality. Frequently, individuals discover that this was transferred to them directly through parental or peer criticism or indirectly through parental repression of the subject or of any discussion of sexuality in the home. Many of our patients have been sexually abused; they experience intense shame regarding these experiences.

In order to better understand the shame experience for compulsive eaters, we present the history of five compulsive eaters who have worked to understand the sources and effects of their shame in order to heal and attain serenity in their personal programs of recovery.

Stacy's Story

Stacy, a 40-year-old bulimic, was married and had two elementary school children when she came to the conclusion that her life was unmanageable physically and emotionally. A full-time mother and homemaker, it was becoming more and more difficult to attend to even the most basic tasks on a day to day basis. Much of the time she felt as though she was walking around in a fog.

When Stacy first contacted the Eating Disorders Recovery Center, her shame was so great that she would not even give her name or an address where information regarding the program could be sent to her. It was almost a month later before she contacted us again. Still refusing to give her name, she made arrangements to come to an information session. Half-jokingly, half-seriously she said we'd recognize her because she'd be the one sitting in the waiting room with a brown paper bag over her head.

Despite her overwhelming shame and tremendous fear of encountering someone she might know, she finally agreed to enter treatment, after much deliberation and discussion with our intake counselor.

Birth Family History

Stacy is the youngest of three daughters. Her father was a first generation immigrant, having come to the United States alone during the Depression. Her mother was an only child of divorced parents. Neither of Stacy's parents has been identified as alcoholic or as a compulsive eater; however, her maternal great-grandmother has been identified as alcoholic.

Stacy's mother and father were staunch Catholics. All the girls attended Catholic schools and participated in the Catholic rites of communion, confession, weekly Sunday Mass, etc. Maintaining a perfect, happy family image was most important to Stacy's parents. They emphasized academic success, good manners and being good.

Stacy does not perceive her parents as very affectionate or demonstrative either with each other or with her or her sisters. The family doctrine was that as long Mother and Father were doing the right things for you, that is, providing food, shelter, clothing, help with homework and religious education, then you should know you were loved. Stacy identified early in treatment that she had always felt fearful around her parents and had never understood why. She also frequently had intense, unexplainable feelings of anger toward her mother though she had never expressed these openly to anyone.

Stacy shared that it was only within the six months prior to her contacting the treatment center that she realized she was bulimic. Even two years previously, when her sister was in treatment for bulimia, Stacy maintained a strong denial and didn't even consider the similarities between what she was doing and what her sister said she had been going through. "It's incredible to me that I could be so supportive of my sister and tell others that I couldn't understand how anyone could do that to themselves — while I myself was putting my *own* head in the toilet. Somehow, what I was doing was *different*. It (bulimia) just wasn't that bad." This strong denial pattern was something that Stacy consistently struggled with throughout the initial weeks of treatment.

In the early stage, Stacy's level of self-disclosure was minimal but she was particularly good at being supportive and helpful to other members of her group. In time, she was able to share more about herself and to see that being a good friend to others was one of the ways she isolated herself and hid her shame. "As long as I can smile and say and do the right thing, no one will suspect how insecure I am. No one will suspect that I am bulimic or that everything is not wonderful in my family."

Stacy has discovered her shame in many elements of her life. "Shame is like a pit, a black hole in my stomach. I feel as though I'm going to sink into it or that it's going to swallow me up. It makes my skin burn. I want to hide. I don't want to look at anyone and I don't want anyone to see me."

Stacy feels shame about almost every aspect of herself and her life. "I'm not productive enough. I'm terribly ashamed that I never finished college and yet deathly afraid of going back. I'm sure I'll fail. I won't look for a job for the same reason. Nothing I do is ever good enough. My shame makes me afraid to try anything but then I'm angry and ashamed of myself for being so lazy and for not trying. I can't win."

Stacy has a litany of life experiences and ways of defining herself which have perpetuated her selfshame for years. Her Shame circle (see Fig.1) is filled with what Stacy perceives as proof of her inadequacy. You can see that Stacy is angry and ashamed about the many standards set up for her that she has not met.

In treatment, Stacy has been encouraged to look at her shame and to explore some of its roots. In completing transgenerational genograms, she was able to look beyond her anger and fear of her parents and to start to see their shame and understand how that was transferred to her.

Stacy was asked to depict her mother's shame and her father's shame. Here is what she came up with:

"I've always had a fearful response to my mother and an intense, unexplainable anger toward her. Even as a child, I'd have dreams of her being like the Wicked Witch of the West. So it was really interesting for me to look beyond this and consider what my mother might be shamed about (see Fig. 2). My mother's mother and family were Catholic. My mother's father was a Protestant and an alcoholic. Mother always told us that *her* mother's family and the Church considered her a bastard, even though she was raised a Catholic. Apparently, Mother's maternal grandmother was alcoholic and was physically and emotionally very abusive to my mother. Her mother (my grandmother) never intervened. It was as if she (my grandmother) was also so ashamed of my mother that she turned her back on her, abandoned her. Mother says she never felt wanted as a child. What's really funny about that is that all the while I was growing up, I never felt that I was wanted either. I guess, just like Mother, I never felt good enough to belong to my family."

Here we see the perfectionistic, idealized belief that there is a certain person or a certain way Stacy and her mother have to be in order to be loved, accepted, nurtured

Figure 1. Stacy's Shame

Figure 2. Mother's Shame

and wanted. Stacy's belief and fear is that if she is not this person, then she leaves herself wide open for abuse from others. It is like deserving to be abused because she doesn't measure up. Stacy was taught this, probably in both direct and indirect ways, by her mother, who had the actual experience of being emotionally abandoned by her mother, her father and her grandmother, then physically abandoned by her father and ridiculed and demeaned by her grandmother. Essentially, Stacy absorbed her mother's unresolved shame.

Stacy remembers her father as a very perfectionistic person. She was afraid of him and her goal as a child was never to do anything to disappoint or displease him.

"I can remember a scene from my childhood that really exemplifies my feelings and my relationship with my father. I was really young. I don't even think I was in school yet. I can remember sitting in the stairwell and hearing my father yelling at my older sister because she was having problems with her math homework. I remember being so hurt by his anger. I don't know why it hurt me so — he wasn't yelling at me. But it felt as though he were. He was calling her stupid, telling her she was lazy. I determined right then that I would never do anything to warrant his yelling at me that way. I made sure I never had any problems with math and spent all my growing-up years doing things that I knew would please him."

When Stacy was asked to draw a picture of her father's shame (see Fig. 3), her focus was on his cultural heritage and lack of education.

"My father arrived in the United States from Ireland when he was 16. Because he was the youngest in his family, he had not been given any education or training in a trade. I know he lived without the presence of a father for much of his early life but I don't know why. Father was very much ashamed of his background and his lack of education. He worked very hard to lose his Irish accent. He was a hard worker and very determined to succeed. I think that part of his inability to accept imperfection or mistakes from my sisters and me is that he saw these as

Figure 3. Father's Shame

a direct reflection on him as a success or a failure. He always maintained that you could do anything if you just put your mind to it. After all, he did. I guess what I can really relate to in looking at my father's shame is his perfectionism. He had such high standards for himself and everyone else. So do I. Even though he worked hard and was successful, he was always ashamed of his lack of education and so am I."

Again, we see in Stacy's life a role model whose personal stance was based on the belief that who you are is never good enough. You must be educated, a hard worker and determined. You must also appear to be flawless. If you don't succeed, it is simply because you are lazy.

Stacy perceives the masculine aspect of herself as the basis of her anger and aggression. She sees the feminine aspect of herself as weak and phony.

Shame Themes

"My aggressiveness is masculine (see Fig. 4). I feel it is expressed inappropriately through my trying always to control other people, especially my children. My aggressiveness is not physical but emotional. I yell and scream. I manipulate through words or certain looks. I am always very ashamed when I act this way toward my children. In my recovery, I've tried to heal this partly by working to be less controlling. I try to encourage my kids to express their feelings. And I've learned to apologize when I know my behavior toward them has been inappropriate.

"My feminine side is weakness (see Fig. 5). I see myself as weak and ineffectual. I isolate myself in my home. If it weren't for the fact that my kids are in school and involved in activities, I'd probably never leave my house. Oh, I put up a good front. I say and do the right things for my neighbors or at the kids' school. But underneath that facade is a scared, immobilized, weak person who is hiding behind the role of wife and mother. I hate this part of me. I'm so ashamed of myself. I feel as if I'm supposed to be doing more but I'm just so afraid that I can't."

Figure 4. Masculinity

Figure 5. Femininity

Stacy, like most of our patients, sees her feminine side as weak, passive and unwanted. This is strikingly similar to her perception of her mother's shame and may explain some of the intense anger she feels toward her mother. Her mother, as the role model or symbol of femininity, is also the target for her anger about what she sees as the negative aspect of herself. Her father's perfectionism and his tendency to base worth of self on accomplishments and behavior further degrade her. Even though Stacy's choice to be an at-home mother might be right in her mother's eyes, it is not *good enough* by her father's standards. But, fearful and ashamed of her aggressiveness, Stacy cannot be comfortable or satisfied with her masculine side either. She sees the aggression and the need to have control over others as abusive and demeaning. This dilemma culminates in Stacy's pervasive sense of immobilization and contributes to a diminished sense of self.

Stacy's selfshame perpetuates her isolation and the isolation perpetuates her selfshame. Her drawing of her own shame is of a woman tied up in a block of ice, with chains binding it (see Fig. 6). "I am so locked up inside myself. I am cold — sometimes unfeeling — to myself and to others — even those I love. I am frozen in my shame. I am dirty, tied up, frozen and chained. I feel stupid and immobilized because the knife to cut the rope, the cable cutter to cut the chain and the soap to clean myself up with are all within my reach. Yet I feel I can't move. I don't know whether it's that I can't or that I won't reach for them. I don't believe I will ever have the courage to move, to live, to love, to feel. There are also matches and sticks inside my wall of ice. These could be used to build a fire to melt the ice I'm frozen inside. But I'm afraid to use them. I'm afraid they might burn me up."

Stacy's selfshame — her isolation and also her anger at herself for not "being more" is reflected in her drawing and the description of her bodyshame (see Fig. 7). Though considered thin and attractive by others, Stacy perceives herself as overweight. Though she says she despises those parts of her body which feel overweight to her, she also

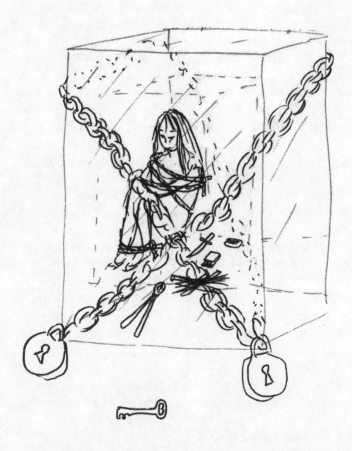

Figure 6. Selfshame

Figure 7. Bodyshame

recognizes that this perception is one more way to keep distance between herself and others. "I feel ashamed of fat anywhere on my body, especially on my hips, around my knees and my upper arms. I feel 50 pounds heavier than I really am. It's as though I have an extended boundary around myself to physically keep other people out. So far in my recovery, I've really tried to reason with myself, to accept that my distorted body image is an extension of how I'm feeling emotionally — not what I really look like. Even though this hasn't made the fat feelings go away completely, it does help me not to get back into my bulimic behaviors. I'm better able to talk myself out of starving myself or beating myself up with a binge/purge episode. I'm also beginning to realize that my hunger is connected to my isolation. When I drew my shame in relation to hunger (see Fig. 8), the stick people represented my hunger to be connected and attached to others. I see that I have a powerful yearning to be close to people. I don't want to be alone and trapped any more! I feel a wall between myself and my husband and children. This makes me very sad. One of the ways I'm working on healing from my shame is by sharing more about my shame feelings with my husband. Those times when I have he has been supportive and helpful. I've also been more honest regarding my thoughts and feelings in group. I try to be more open and honest with my children about my disease and why I have acted so crazy sometimes."

Stacy exemplifies the idealization of the one-sided masculine-oriented principles of control and perfection. She idealizes accomplishments, being able to do everything on your own and the notion of being able to accomplish anything you make up your mind to. Being acceptable as a person is based on doing certain things, on thinking and acting the right way.

When Stacy began treatment she was filled with unexplainable shame. At first she felt her shamefulness was about her imperfect body and her loss of control over her binge/purge behaviors. Though these are the bodyshame themes for Stacy, underlying these are the selfshame

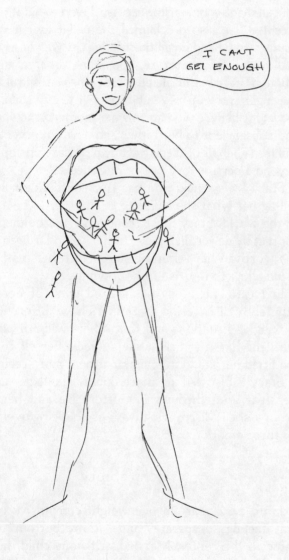

Figure 8. Hunger

themes which focus on the conflict between her masculine and feminine sides. Stacy has idealized her father, who believed that being emotionally independent, determined, educated and monetarily successful were what it took to be accepted. He also proclaimed the belief that if you didn't manage to be and do all these things, it was simply because you were lazy; therefore, you didn't deserve any better. Though Stacy has idealized these principles, she also resents the anger and fear they subjected her to as a child. Her role model for being a woman was her mother, who was passive and subservient to her father and never intervened on the children's behalf or displayed any physical signs of affection beyond a perfunctory kiss on the cheek.

Stacy feels stuck. She has two conflicting role models telling her what she needs to be in order to be acceptable to the world. Stacy must resolve her masculine/feminine conflict by de-idealizing her father's standards and finding the worth in her feminine side, which her mother never could allow to flourish in her own life.

In treatment, Stacy has shared more of herself with others. By discovering that others have different ways of looking at situations and that others will not punish her with the harsh criticism she subjects herself to, she has modified her standards, making them more realistic.

Stacy is also talking more openly about her anger and her fear and, through her after-care and her support groups, she is discovering ways of not being overwhelmed by these emotions.

John's Story

John, a 32-year-old overweight compulsive overeater, was feeling "desperate" and "at my bottom" when he came to the center. Married, with one child, he and his wife had discussed his ongoing obsession with food and dieting for some time before he decided to seek counseling assistance. His wife was very supportive of his decision to enter treatment and participated in the Family Program.

An intelligent and creative individual, John had been on many diet and exercise programs throughout his adult life. But no matter what he tried, he never sustained his weight loss for very long. Since John never had a problem with his weight as a youngster or adolescent, he approached his weight problem for years as simply a response to stress from work or to poor eating and exercise habits. But as his repeated attempts to diet away his overweight failed, he began to look more within himself. He realized that there was something emotional and spiritual connected to his compulsive eating.

Birth Family History

John is the second child and oldest son of a strong Catholic family of German heritage. There were three girls and two boys in his family. John and his family had lived in a blue collar neighborhood in a Midwestern city. The family lived the traditional family lifestyle of the 1950s, with father, as head of the household, going off to work every day and mother staying at home to take care of the house and the children. The family went to church every Sunday and the father was very active in church organizations, so he was frequently out at night. All the children attended Catholic schools.

John felt that he, as the oldest son, was expected to emulate his father in every way.

There is no alcoholism identified in the family history but in the course of treatment, John identified his mother as a compulsive overeater and he has examined more closely the family's perception of her as depressed, fragile and needing to be insulated from the outside world.

Shame Themes

John has come to see that his selfshame and bodyshame are interconnected closely with his sexuality and his sense of what it is to be masculine and to be feminine. John represents the struggle that men face in not living up to the ideal masculine image.

During his participation in one of the Shame Workshops, John drew his shame as residing in his chest and eyes (see Fig. 9). His depiction of his sexuality is located in the same body parts, particularly the chest and torso (see Fig. 10). This body area is also the aspect of his body that John is the most ashamed of and uncomfortable with (see Fig. 11). Interestingly enough, this is also where he indicates his femininity resides. This suggests that John's selfshame is connected to his sexuality and his struggle to accept his feminine side as an attractive, acceptable aspect of himself.

"My shame is sexual and I feel it in my eyes and chest. I cannot look people in the eyes for long — and not at all when I'm pouring out my heart. I am frequently ashamed of my moodiness and am especially ashamed when I cry or express anger. Though I am proud of being sensitive, compassionate and creative, I am most often embarrassed by my emotions. In my birth family, at school and now at work, I show little emotion. As a kid at home, we were encouraged to share opinions but feelings were seldom mentioned. It was unacceptable to be out of step and a lot of feelings were hidden. I believe we were a morals-bound family. If something went wrong, it was someone's fault. If you got in trouble, you had done something you shouldn't have and deserved the consequences. Nobody cut much slack for anyone else.

"Even though I never experienced any direct physical sexual abuse, I believe that I experienced sexual abuse through my family's and my religion's attitudes and feelings about sex. Sexuality was repressed and any expression of it was shamed in my family.

"I've been ashamed of my body at least since puberty. I went to great lengths to avoid taking physical education in high school because I dreaded the thought of having to be shirtless in front of others." (John doesn't perceive his chest and torso as measuring up to the ideal male body image as square and muscular but thinks of it as soft and rounded.)

"My shame feelings have always had to do with my chest, nipples and torso. I also remember feeling the need

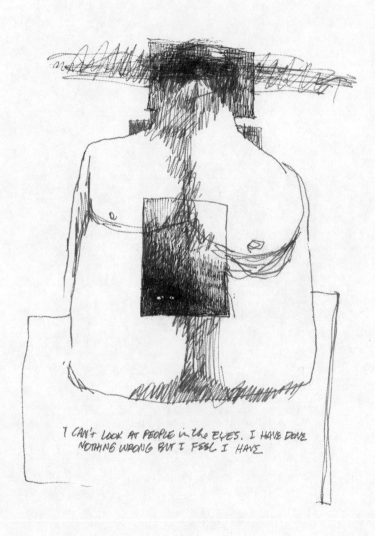

Figure 9. John's Shame

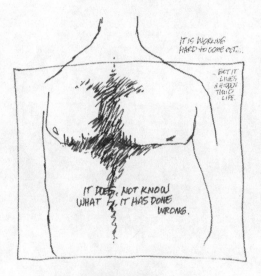

MY SEXUALITY

IT IS WORKING
HARD TO COME OUT...

.. BUT IT
LIVES
A HIDDEN
TRAILED
LIFE.

IT DOES, NOT KNOW
WHAT IT, IT HAS DONE
WRONG.

MY SEXUALITY IS LOCATED IN MY TORSO.
IT IS AFRAID OF BEING EXPOSED. IT IS AFRAID
OF SPIRITUALITY. IT IS TENDER and CONFUSED.
IT LOOKS FOR NURTURANCE.

Figure 10. John's Sexuality

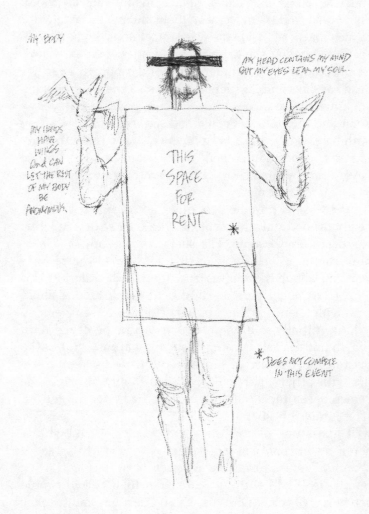

Figure 11. John's Body

to be secretive regarding any romances or dating as a teenager, even with my siblings.

"I was deeply ashamed when my mother found my stash of 'dirty' magazines hidden in my tiny bedroom. She would find them, remove them and never say a word to me. The ache inside me was tremendous. I would walk around knowing she knew — and I knew that she knew. Mom could carry a thunderstorm of disapproval over her head for days and its silent fury was so shame-provoking and unrelenting. I don't know how I coped. I just stayed as quiet and invisible as I could and slinked around. Usually nothing was ever said. I also knew at these times that my father had been informed of my transgression but he never said anything either. I always interpreted his silence as disapproval of me."

When asked how he saw other adolescent boys in his neighborhood and school coping with their sexuality, John's responses were vague. His shame, apparently, had kept him from even being able to find out how his peers were learning about themselves and their bodies during this vital transitional period. He doesn't recall talking about girls with friends or even girl-watching as a teenager.

John initially said he didn't know how he coped with the shame he felt coming from his parents. But as he became more aware of himself and his ways of interacting with others, particularly in his family of origin, he remembered incidents in which he had tried to get out from under his shame.

"I guess one of the ways I did cope with the shame about my sexuality as a teenager was to try to spread it around. I remember being ashamed of myself for ratting on my brother. I'm three years older than he and I could see him struggling with his sexual questions and teenage issues. Twice, I told my parents about his drinking beer with his friends and finding *his* stash of dirty magazines in the bedroom we shared. I was ashamed that I hadn't talked to him about these things; I had acted moralistically and insensitively toward him. I had done to him what my mother did to me, bringing disapproval down on him while he lay helplessly in his shame. I have always hated the part of me that did this. As part of healing my shame in recovery, I finally apologized to him."

This is a good example of how shame is transmitted among family members. John was made to feel ashamed of his sexuality and budding sexual interests by parents who were most likely uncomfortable and ashamed of their own. Overwhelmed and feeling helpless in his own shame, John tried to rise above it and to redeem himself by shaming his brother.

In many dysfunctional, shame-based families, the members try to redeem themselves by working at being perfect and by shaming or controlling other family members. Rather than reducing the shame, this action generally makes the shamer even more ashamed of himself for treating someone else in a way that further threatens the interpersonal bridge between himself and the other person.

Despite the fact that John has always seen himself as accepting and appreciative of his feminine side, he has come to realize that he does experience ambivalence regarding many of his more feminine qualities such as expressing emotions. He has also come to recognize that the feminine and masculine aspects of himself seem to be at odds and need reconciliation (see Fig. 12).

"I know that I have kept much of the feminine aspect of myself hidden in a closet, hidden from others. I guess I have been afraid of the ridicule or rejection I may receive from others for being less rational, more emotional. Even though I feel very much a man, I have realized through my drawings and group input that my masculinity does not know who it is. It stands there boldly in front of me but doesn't understand itself. I've always seen my masculinity as being quietly supportive of my femininity, just as I always saw my father being supportive and protective of my mother. Now, though, I wonder if it isn't simply a vagueness about understanding the masculine aspects of myself. I would love to have a well-defined torso, a sleek and muscular chest and muscled abdomen. I would like more muscular upper

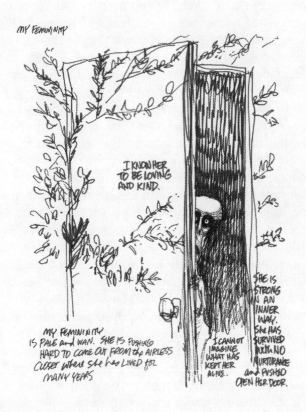

Figure 12. John's Femininity

arms. The reason that having my body look that way is so important to me probably is that on some level, a good looking body symbolizes, to me, the resolution of the emotional/sexual conflicts I feel. I realize now that I would like to feel more manly, more strongly masculine."

John's selfshame focuses on not being entirely able to be the nonsexual being that his parents indicated he needed to be in order to be an acceptable human being. His inability to rise above his physical self and normal sexual feelings left him feeling inadequate as an individual and created a distrust between his inner self and his body.

Throughout this book we have focused on the female experience of the idealization of the masculine. John is not alone in his feelings since many of the men we have treated have expressed similar conflicts regarding their masculinity and femininity.

In John's family the idealized male was his father, who was the head of the household, the protector of women and children and the primary means of support. But in John's community, masculinity also symbolized being athletic, being able to hold your alcohol, being physically strong so you could do physical labor and being interested in sex. The community's concept of masculinity and John's family example of masculinity were similar in some ways (strong, independent, decisive, head of the family) but very different in the physical and sexual realm. John's parents, especially his father who was unable to address sexuality openly with John, left him feeling ashamed and cut off from this aspect of himself. Since John idealized his father, he set out to be like him in both the masculine and feminine way his father had been: creative, gently supportive of mother (women), charitable and quiet (feminine qualities), yet rational, strong, independent, decisive and self-confident (masculine qualities). This idealization left no room for John to explore his more natural masculine/feminine aspects around sexuality, emotional intimacy and expression of emotion. John's shame stems from his desire, his need for these aspects of himself which do not fit into his ideal image of what a man should be.

In his efforts to heal his shame, John has done many things. He has focused on and has had much success with extracting himself from the family of origin role he played, especially with his mother. He has encouraged her to be more independent and he no longer plays the role of protector.

In his relationship with his wife, who has been working diligently on her own program of recovery, they talk openly about the things he has felt ashamed of and they have slowly and lovingly begun to explore their sexual and emotional relationship.

Through the use of guided imagery, John has also explored his relationship with his body and has committed to a program of affirmation, balanced eating and regular exercise to make this relationship more positive, less threatening and shame-provoking.

Rita's Story

Rita, a 30-year-old compulsive overeater, had been involved in individual counseling in an effort to improve her extremely low self-esteem. She decided to come to the treatment center to address her compulsive overeating and weight problem because in her individual counseling she had come to understand how both were barriers to feeling better about herself. She also feared that her overeating and overweight were damaging her relationship with her husband and her children. She knew they were tired of her erratic mood swings and embarrassed by her excessive weight.

Birth Family History

Rita is the second child and second daughter of a family of four children. She describes her mother as very religious, an individual who devoted all her time and attention to her home and her children. She remembers her father as an extremely domineering, rigid man who rarely communicated with the family and walked around with a cloud of anger over his head.

Neither of Rita's parents have been identified as alcoholic or having problems with food or weight. Rita did discover as an adult that her paternal grandfather was an alcoholic who had sexually abused her father's sister and niece. She also recently learned that her father, as the oldest sibling, had quit school to support the family because his father was not able to. Rita's mother had shared with her that she herself never felt she had a mother to talk with or to help her because her mother (Rita's maternal grandmother) spent many years in a tuberculosis sanatorium.

Here we have the setting for a family system whose adult guides were two individuals each of whom had suffered significant emotional losses and probably physical losses as well in their youth. From what Rita has been able to learn, neither of her parents was ever given much nurturance or support in childhood, adolescence or adulthood, to cope with these early losses.

Rita's parents lived a traditional married lifestyle. Dad was the breadwinner and decision-maker and Mom was the homemaker. Rita remembers, "I don't recall seeing much affection or concern between the two of them. Dinner was always on the table when Dad walked in the door. Mom worried if he was late. I can recall a few times when Dad put his arm around Mom as she was doing the dishes but generally, I never saw or heard any expression of love or caring. My father has never said 'I love you' to any of us. Mom says she understands and accepts this. He can't do anything wrong in her eyes but I resent that he could never tell me he loves me. Mother demonstrated affection for me with hugs and kisses and by listening to me when we talked after school but this was all offset by her controlling behaviors toward me and my body as I grew older. None of us kids were ever allowed to express any feelings or opinions that were different from what they (my parents) wanted us to have."

What Rita has identified in her family of origin is a family system based in shame. Children who experience significant breaks in the interpersonal bridge with their primary caretakers frequently suffer feelings of abandonment. These feelings are often interpreted by children as meaning that they aren't good enough to deserve the relationship. The feeling that many children have in these situations are frequently exacerbated by being blamed for the parents' withdrawal or by being told by other adults that they shouldn't feel any anger, sadness or loss. Her description of her parents and their backgrounds, combined with their way of raising Rita and her siblings, are indicative of a family attempting to make up for the past by controlling the present and the future.

Shame Themes

In her efforts to understand her shame as a contributing factor in her disease, Rita has discovered that her inner shame focuses on wanting to be her own person — different from the quiet, caretaking, passive, reclusive, nonsexual individual her parents wanted her to be — and on not being more assertive, courageous and independent.

"I am ashamed of my inability to be assertive, my inability to be independent and my inability to be perfect — to be all the things I think I should be."

Rita's bodyshame focuses on her excess weight and her sexuality; the latter especially became a subject of shaming by her parents at the onset of puberty.

"My mother told me I was fat. She was embarrassed by my changes into womanhood. I was always made to wear hand-me-down clothes that were not in style. I was told to dress modestly in order to hide my cleavage. I was ashamed and embarrassed around my peers. I also was not allowed to wear make-up or nylons, shave my legs or do any of the other things that girls my age were doing. I was not allowed to decide where I wanted to go. Mom took me everywhere and picked me up afterward. They frequently told me they didn't like the few friends I had, who were all outcasts like me. I felt there was something wrong with me for wanting to shave my legs, wear make-up, etc., because I believed Mom must know what was right for me.

"I always used to play football with the boys, as a kid. When I was about 13, Mom told me I couldn't play anymore because I was a young woman now and it wouldn't be right for me to play now that I had breasts. I still wanted to play but felt bad for wanting to. I was angry at Mom but I turned the anger on myself. I got angry at my body for making me different and taking away from me something I enjoyed. I was angry at my inner self for wanting to do something I obviously wasn't supposed to want to do anymore.

"My parents interpreted my desire to be different from what they wanted — wanting to wear nice clothes, make-up and so on — as rebellion. They told me and my brother and sisters that I was bad and encouraged them to stay away from me after I left home."

Here we see a good example of how a parent's shame and fear of sexuality and a growing child's need to expand her interests and energies beyond the family system can create an atmosphere of oppression, confusion and alienation, a breaking of the interpersonal bridge between parent and child. Rita's interest in growing up was quite natural for a young girl entering puberty. Her desire to be involved in activities with a little less parental intervention and to do the same kinds of things that her female peers were doing, like wearing make-up, was met with such parental disapproval that she questioned her goodness as a person for wanting the very things her parents said were bad and therefore forbidden to her.

In many ways Rita's parents sexualized all her desires to be more independent. Consequently, Rita's selfshame became intricately attached to her perception of and her relationship with her body. She grew up feeling bad in relation to her parents' standards of goodness and morality. She felt ostracized, different and therefore unacceptable in relation to her peers. This has left Rita feeling unworthy and unable to reach out to others.

As a part of a Shame Workshop experience, Rita described her shame as being like a circle of flame that surrounds and imprisons her (see Fig. 13).

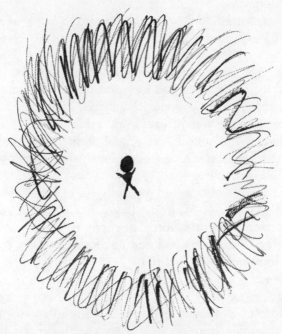

Figure 13. Rita's Shame

"I see myself stuck in the fire. I can feel its heat, the burning sensation on my skin. I am in the center of the ring of fire. I'm filled with good feelings yet too vulnerable to get free from the flames. This is how I feel in relationships and even in social situations, as though I want to reach out, to be connected but, I can't. I keep wishing and waiting for others to come to me.

"The shame I feel about my body and my sexuality is similar. The shame is a hot, burning sensation. I see my body (see Fig. 14) as a fat, scarred, imperfect blob. Hot shame burns both on the outside and the inside. I have always felt ashamed of my weight, my body odor and my need for sexual pleasure.

"Sex (see Fig. 15) is all mixed up for me. Because of the strong negative messages from my parents about my physical sexual features and my desire to go out, wear make-up, etc. as an adolescent, I have always felt ashamed of my desire and need for sexual closeness. I need intimacy,

Figure 14. Rita's Body

Figure 15. Rita's Sexuality

feeling connected, yet I am ashamed and afraid of this need. Again, the shame is like a burning sensation that goes all around and all through me."

Rita's conflict regarding her masculine and feminine sides is a result of the shame of both her mother and her father which she feels. However, she tends to be more ashamed of the feminine aspect of herself. This is probably because her mother was her idealized parent for many years and because of the close link between her feminine side and her sexuality. In her picture of her mother's shame (see Fig. 16), Rita's perception of her mother is of a sponge. The circle of shame binds everyone in the family to her mother and binds her mother inside the circle of shame as well.

"Mom is like a sponge. She soaks her identity from us. While she has taken her identity from us, she also took ours from us. She lives through us, making us dependent on her meeting our needs. She kept us tied to her emotionally by not teaching us to meet our own needs and by rescuing us from ourselves. There was no chance to make mistakes as we were growing up so it's hard to make a mistake as an adult.

"The piece of my femininity that I'm most ashamed about is what I perceive to be my inability to take for myself and give to others in a healthy way. My mother never directly asked for what she needed or pursued what she needed. She was always other-focused. Consequently, she appeared to me to be unable to listen to others and to give to others in a healthy way. This is what feels most shameful to me about my mother and myself.

"In my depiction of my father's shame (see Fig. 17), I see someone who is not quite a person, a 'dumb bell'. He is full of anger. It is a weight he walks around with. It makes him somewhat unreachable. It keeps the world at arm's length so he cannot be hurt and let the anger explode. I feel ashamed of his anger, his inability to have friends, to allow others their own opinion and of his inability to say 'I love you.' In myself, I am ashamed of similar things. I'm ashamed of my difficulty in reaching out to others because

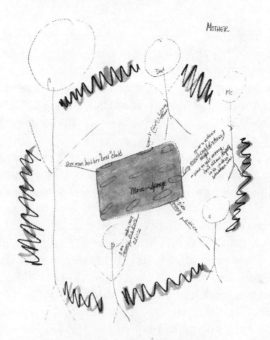

Figure 16. Rita's Mother's Shame

Figure 17. Rita's Father's Shame

I feel inferior or different. I am ashamed of my own anger but also of my lack of assertiveness. I avoid closeness and I am sometimes harshly judgmental of other people. I know now that this is simply a way to protect myself by keeping other people at some psychological or physical distance. But all it really does is make me feel more inferior and ashamed."

For Rita, the healing of her shame has come as she is better able to forgive herself for not being perfect (according to her parents' standards) and as she can accept as natural her interest in friendships and in sexuality. An intelligent and introspective woman, Rita has already grasped many insights into her anger and fear and she is working to separate herself from her parents' shame as it was expressed through their anger, fear and rigidity.

Rita has made a strong commitment to practicing assertiveness with others, especially at work, where authority figures tend to remind her of her father. She has made a sincere effort to speak up, not to hide, in group sessions and has established relationships with some recovering people outside the group experience.

While she is working to be more accepting of her need to feel connected to others, she has also taken many steps to be less enabling with her husband and less people-pleasing with her parents. Honestly recognizing her conflicts about intimacy and sexuality, she has encouraged her husband to participate in marital counseling, which they now are involved in on a weekly basis.

What is most important is that as Rita has become more comfortable with her anger (a piece of her masculine side) and her need to be connected to others (a piece of her feminine side), she has found more self-forgiveness. She understands that being angry does not have to carry with it the threat of disconnecting yourself from others, as her father did or that wanting to be connected to others doesn't necessarily mean losing yourself by focusing all your energy and attention on others, like her mother.

She sees that she is not very different from others. She can even laugh at herself at times and has begun to contemplate the notion that being happy is more fulfilling than being right (being perfect).

Maria's Story

Maria was 28 years old, married and pregnant with her second child when she came to the Eating Disorders Recovery Center looking for help for her bulimia. She reported that she had never been overweight or underweight as a child or adolescent. Her bulimia flared up during her first year in college when she was having a tremendously difficult time adjusting to being away from home and was unsuccessful at making friends.

When Maria began treatment, she at first experienced an emotional dilemma when asked to talk about her family of origin. To her, she had a wonderful childhood and could not imagine any connection between her experiences growing up and her bulimia or the way she felt about herself now.

However, as Maria listened to others, she realized that examining family history and relationships did not mean blaming. She was then able to talk more openly regarding her early family history.

Birth Family History

Maria is the youngest of four children who grew up in a nice, upper middle-class suburb. Her father's family emigrated from Italy, something she believed her father was extremely proud of. Maria identified her father as a compulsive overeater who was overweight. Her mother was considered a beautiful woman, tall and slender, whose weight never fluctuated and who was always full of energy and at ease with others.

Maria recalls the focus of the relationship with her mother was " . . . to please her, to stay out of her hair, not to mess things up and to avoid conflict." Maria hated the arguments she had heard between her mother and her older brothers and sisters and she had determined to avoid these arguments with her mother. "The rule I tried to live by was: *Be a good girl*. I always tried to do what she thought I should do. Affection and concern were expressed by hugs, kisses, encouragement to participate in activities. But I didn't feel much warmth there. Mom always wanted outward appearances to be just right but she never seemed to let this stop her from doing anything she wanted to do.

"My relationship with my father was a little different. When I was small, I followed him around. He always helped me with anything I needed and was available to do anything for me. I realize now that sometimes that availability was more physical than emotional, though I know he tried. My father was extremely concerned that none of us kids should ever be compared with the others or anyone else. Apparently, he was critically compared to his brother by his father when he was growing up. I think this left my dad with a pervasive feeling of not being good enough. He would often say he wasn't a good enough father, even though, from my way of looking at it, he was always giving to us, giving us time, attention, money and trying to show us love."

Maria's description of her family indicates that her father carried a deep sense of selfshame. His compulsive eating was most likely a tool to sedate his feelings of inferiority. Though Maria cannot perceive any blatant shame themes for her mother, her mother's perfectionism seems to have sent a message, at least to Maria, that being perfect is important to being valued as a person and as a woman. According to Maria this was never directly communicated through criticism or ridicule from her parents but rather it was implied by their attitudes, interactions and encouragement.

"Both my parents would let me know they were proud of me. Looking back, I realize I sometimes felt pressured to get involved; that it was most important that I play the piano, dance and sew. Sometimes I enjoyed it and sometimes I didn't. But Mom always encouraged me to be involved and I think Dad lived through our activities. This was a source of pride for him.

"I don't recall either of my parents criticizing my body. I think Dad thought it was fine and Mom did tell me I had a cute shape. I do remember my older sister always thought she was too fat, even though she was very thin. She would taunt me about my body and body processes. All my siblings made fun of my body at times, especially after I hit adolescence. They used to call me Jello Bottom. I've never felt comfortable in a bathing suit and I spent a lot of time making up excuses so I wouldn't have to go swimming with friends."

Maria's story is a good example of how shame and consequently perfectionism can be transmitted through *perfect* families. These are families where the parents' way of caring and nurturing their children is not necessarily negative or critical but whose own expectations or ways of coping with any shame they may have of their own is transmitted and, therefore, absorbed as normal by the family members.

Shame Themes

When asked to depict her shame, Maria drew a hollow tree trunk in a field of flowers (see Fig.18).

"My shame brings up many feelings. It makes me feel invisible, void, empty, ignored, alone, unworthy, worthless, violated, unimportant and transparent. When I experience shame, I feel it in my stomach and in my face.

"A definite internal shame theme for me is not being good enough at tasks. I seem to have an overriding sense that the things I do could be done better by anyone else. I also feel ashamed of myself for not being a more interesting person, more sociable, etc."

It is interesting that Maria's inner shame themes are consistent with the way she describes her father and very much in contrast to how she saw her mother. Her mother's energy, sociability and her tall, slender body seem to be what was idealized by the family, at least by Maria. Her inability to be like her mother in these ways may be one of the roots of Maria's internal and external shame. Her siblings' teasing about her development, her mother's beauty and the family emphasis on doing the right thing made Maria feel hollow and inept.

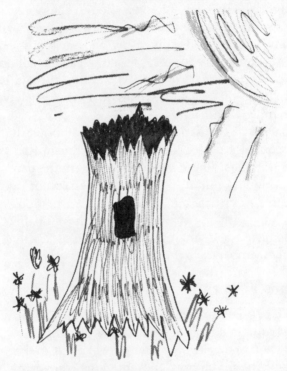

Figure 18. Maria's Shame

"I realize now that somewhere along the way I failed to learn to nurture my inner self. I guess I was too afraid of conflict or of upsetting the apple cart to even say what I needed. Since I never found the way to nurture myself on the inside, I emphasized my exterior as being the most important."

In exploring feelings about femininity in one of the Shame Workshops, Maria shared that she is very comfortable and proud of her feminine side and of being female. "I see my femininity as being like a patchwork quilt. (see Fig. 19) To me, femininity is softness, strength, comfort, nurturance, support and warmth. It provides connection and wisdom. It is a source of perseverance, survival and coping, passed down from one generation to the next."

Figure 19. Maria's Femininity

Yet, as proud as Maria is of her femininity, she has also come to identify it as a source of shame for her, at times. "I feel that the feminine aspect is the more dominant side of me. In some situations, this is wonderful. In others, it doesn't allow for self-preservation. I sometimes get so caught up in my role as wife and mother that I lose myself. I become a martyr."

Maria's selfshame has focused on wanting to be the perfect person. Yet, because she was not always internally able to be, or even want to be the epitome of perfection that she felt her parents believed in, she overemphasized her body and emphasized doing the right things as a way to be acceptable.

In recovery, Maria has had to learn to identify her worth as a person and to let go of her old standards of perfection. Overall, she has become more accepting of her body, looking at it now more as a reflection of her inner

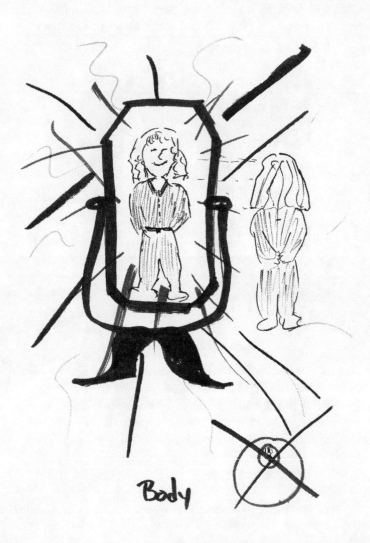

Body

Figure 20. Maria's Recovery

beauty and a sign of her recovery (see Fig. 20). Her bodyshame is not completely gone, though. She still feels ashamed of a face scar and of blemishes when they occur. But now, most of the bodyshame is from the "scars" her bulimia has left behind: lined lips, broken blood vessels, swollen glands.

Her need to be all-caring and all-giving in order to be acceptable and connected to others is changing. "I now realize that before my recovery, I would do almost anything to become attached to someone. Now, I'm beginning to see that, though attachment and connections are important, they can't be paid for by losing myself."

Maria has had to work hard to accept the fact that if her husband is angry or upset, it's not her job to fix it; that as a mother with two small children, her house is not always going to be immaculate. She's had to be assertive with her family of origin, learning that they won't hate her or be disappointed in her if she doesn't come to visit every time they want her to. She has also been learning how to be angry and to express her anger rather than "swallowing it."

A significant piece in Maria's recovery has been the process of "turning it over" by reaching out to other recovering people by phone, by regularly attending support groups and by allowing herself to develop a more loving and forgiving relationship with her Higher Power. "Many times during the week, especially when I'm home alone and the kids have been cranky, it's a phone call to someone or just talking to my Higher Power that saves me from the self-negativity I could get into that always leads me back into my disease."

Michelle's Story

Michelle was a divorced, single parent in her mid-thirties when she sought treatment for her compulsive over-eating. Michelle reported that she had been overweight since childhood. As an adult, she had periods of success at losing weight and, one time, she even kept her excess weight off for about two years. Initially, the most difficult aspect of accepting her disease, was that there just isn't anything logical about it. She knew what to do and how to eat in order to lose weight, so why couldn't she just do it?

Birth Family History

Michelle was the oldest of three children born to well educated, socially conscious, fairly liberal parents. Though neither of her siblings have been identified as having eating disorders, Michelle has identified that her father was a compulsive overeater and that her mother was alcoholic.

Her mother's alcoholism and resulting depression was the primary issue in the family unit. Her maternal grandmother was alcoholic as well.

"My relationship with my mother was erratic and difficult. When she was drinking, she would want to hug, kiss hello and goodbye, etc. When she was sober, she was domineering and controlling and insisted on always being right. She would acknowledge my feelings by listening to what I had to say, then tell me that I was wrong and that I really felt another way.

"I think my mother, in many ways, was ashamed of herself constantly. Her mother (my maternal grandmother) was very concerned about appearances and I think my mother was acutely aware of falling short of my grandmother's vision of the family and daughter she wanted. To a lesser degree, I think my mother wanted our family to be perfect. Nothing was ever quite right about her life or herself, as she saw it. My mother was always the right weight. She dressed immaculately and was very concerned about her appearance. She didn't like her large, bony hands or muscular upper arms. I doubt she ever felt good about her body.

"She thought I was overweight and she was always after me to lose weight. She sometimes commented negatively about certain body parts, like my stomach, legs, etc., and even tried to pay me 'incentives' to lose weight.

"My relationship with my mother was a mix of contradictions. She would show concern for me by trying to do something to help and affection by doing something for or giving something to me. She'd unquestioningly give or do anything. Yet she was critical of my body, critical of my feelings and always told me that I didn't finish anything. I remember feeling that I probably wouldn't succeed in many things."

As Michelle continued in treatment, her perceptions about her mother became less jumbled and judgmental. When asked to depict her mother's shame, Michelle drew a woman covered with dirt, with a few flowers attempting to sprout here and there. She was separated from her three children (see Fig. 21). "I recognize now that my mother was sad, lonely and ashamed. She had no self-confidence; she could be warm but was often unavailable. She had lots of barriers around herself — to hide her shame, I guess. Consequently, she came across as self-absorbed. She was always right, never wrong. I realize that I have felt ashamed of her for having so many problems and for acting so strongly aggressive and opinionated when she was, in reality, the opposite of the strongly assertive, always right person that she worked so hard to look like."

Figure 21. Michelle's Mother's Shame

Michelle's role model of femininity is a woman with much shame who attempted to cover this by being masculine, that is, strong, opinionated, controlling. It would be reasonable to assume that Michelle's mother took this masculine stance because she had been taught to perceive these traits as a sign of perfection and therefore of goodness.

In exploring her relationship with her father, Michelle's feelings and perceptions have changed in the course of her recovery. Initially, she saw him as the stable parent who could be depended upon to be practical. But as Michelle has been able to be more open-minded about herself and her own issues, she has come to see that, though she idealized him and saw him as the perfect parent, he is rigid in many of his attitudes, tending to see things as right or wrong and he has also tended to be emotionally inaccessible (see Fig. 22).

"I see my father as warm, though he seldom shows it. He has always been busy with work and he strongly believes in always being productive, in not wasting anything. My father occasionally showed affection by hugging me. Demonstrating concern was just as difficult. I remember him looking agitated and walking away, as though he couldn't cope with the fact that something was bothering me. He would do whatever he could to help but often at my mother's urging.

"My father weighed himself and charted his weight every day for years so I guess he must have had real concerns about his weight. I know that my mother would get after him about it. He never said anything about my body or my weight but I can guess that I have been diminished in his eyes because of the way he feels about overweight women. His first comment about any woman is her weight and figure."

Both of Michelle's parents emphasized the more masculine-oriented principles of appearances, doing the right thing and being logical and practical. Certain emotions were acceptable, others were not. Michelle's excessive weight was seen as a problem to be fixed.

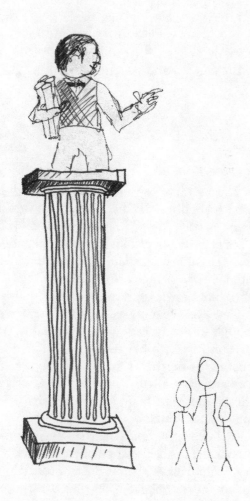

Figure 22. Michelle's Father's Shame

Shame Themes

In talking about her shame, Michelle drew a picture of a barrier, with barbs and fire beneath it (see Fig. 23). "I feel my shame in my stomach. It's a heavy solid blob of wet cardboard or something like that which has a density and thickness almost impossible to get through. The underneath is barbed and frantic and full of anxiety. Sometimes that part seeps out but most often it's held in check by the density and weight above it.

Figure 23. Michelle's Shame

"I know I have never felt good enough and I know that in both childhood and adolescence I felt shame for being overweight. When I was married, my husband used to make statements of fact about the negative aspects of my body. He didn't complain or tease, he just made offhand comments in a matter-of-fact way. I always felt subhuman, that he was right and justified in his opinions."

Here we see how selfshame and never feeling good enough interconnects with bodyshame. Michelle's erratic relationship with her mother left her uncertain and untrusting of her inner self-perception. Her mother's criticism and attempts to "fix" Michelle's weight increased the uncertainty and bound together the selfshame and the bodyshame. Both became sources of inferiority feelings.

Michelle has identified that her shame resides in her stomach. This is also the body area of which she feels the most ashamed — the pit of her stomach, where she feels her mother "resides." Michelle's description of her shame and her perception of how her mother hid her own shame are very similar — a barrier with intense emotions underneath. As Michelle becomes more comfortable with her emotions and can feel more forgiving toward her mother, the intensity of this shame will decrease.

In identifying her internal shame themes, Michelle states, "I feel shame that I can't handle life situations effortlessly. I tend to think that other people are competent and comfortable in all situations and I feel inferior because I'm not. I think I should be feminine and strong, competent and vulnerable, all things at all times. Therefore, I never *internally* feel right. It's a no-win situation all the time. Of course, these feelings are in the background most of the time. I can see that I've handled many situations as correctly or as competently as possible, but underneath I always second-guess myself."

Michelle recognizes that she really is conflicted over wanting to be feminine, yet seeing femininity as weak and, therefore, undesirable.

"My image of myself is of a feisty little person inside my soft, round, overweight exterior. That person is solid muscle, a woman but a hard, nonfeminine woman. In some ways, I admire her for having more power and strength than I do. I don't like that she's nonfeminine, though. Feisty, strong and powerful isn't compatible, for me, with being feminine, nice and lovable. On the other hand, femininity is synonymous with being weak, unprepared, scared, unable to cope and capable of being victimized."

Michelle's contradictory perceptions of what it is to be feminine come from both her mother's contradictory behavior and society's contradictory messages. The common concept of femininity in our masculinized culture is that women should be kind, loving, generous caretakers — but then they are also seen as *less than* for being that way rather than being aggressive, rational and independent. This is a difficult set of conflicting messages for both men and women. It leaves many people with the feeling that they must find a way to be strong in all the qualities and characteristics that anyone can have, just to be considered an adequate human being.

As Michelle has continued in her treatment and recovery, she has worked hard to be less critical and judgmental of herself. She has become more comfortable being at home alone and no longer feels overwhelmed with guilt if she is not always working — like her father.

Michelle has been given permission through group and her individual treatment sessions to identify and share the emotions, interests and values she has which do not strictly conform to the right-or-wrong, achievement-oriented, always practical upbringing she had.

As she has started to modify her idealization of her father, now seeing him as more human, and as she has been able to see her mother's struggle with the same kind of issues that she herself has faced, Michelle reports that she is becoming more and more comfortable with the feminine aspect of herself.

"I'm glad I'm a woman. Women have value and the qualities that I most value. I believe my masculine side has been well developed as part of my survival instinct but I'm discovering how much more I value a lot of the people-oriented, feminine traits. I'm least proud that women aren't more like men in the areas of being assertive and valuing themselves. What I'm trying to learn is a comfortable blending of the two."

Personal Reflections On
Bodyshame And Sexual Abuse

In a previous chapter, the trauma of sexual abuse was discussed as a factor in the development of shame about the body and we said that many survivors of sexual abuse later develop eating disorders.

In both John's and Rita's stories, we saw how sexual repression and negativity by parents regarding the sexual development of young adolescents can result in their developing intensely shameful feelings regarding their sexuality, their desire and need to express sexual curiosity and interest in their bodies in general.

At the treatment center, we have also had survivors of incest, rape and molestation. Following are two pictures regarding their bodies that women who were sexually abused have shared in the Shame Workshops.

In Sonni's picture (see Fig. 24), she describes a soft young girl/woman. "On the outside, she is soft, pink and aromatic, like a pretty pink rose. But on the inside she feels **black**. It's like a black hole: deep, empty, a never-ending tunnel. There is intense pain. She is trying to hide her eyes, so the covering over her face and eyes is also black. Her body is filth to her — every part that was touched by all the dirty, disgusting sex that she had — thousands of times — out of anger and hatred and groping for what she thought was love. She feels she has no right to the real thing."

Sonni and her family were abandoned by her father when she was five years old. The youngest of five children, she was emotionally lost and neglected by a mother who was overwhelmed by her own shame of being divorced and a family struggling to survive. In her teens, she got into drugs. She was raped one time while stoned. Her intense shame for being abandoned and then raped led her to a pattern of promiscuity — trading sex for drugs. This intensified her shame, however. For many years, as an adolescent, she starved herself to punish herself and her body. In her early twenties, as she was trying to get off drugs and get herself together, she compulsively overate and became overweight. "I realize now," she says, "that this was a way to insulate myself from my sexuality and my pain. I didn't want to feel sexually vulnerable to anyone again."

Sonni was bulimic, binging and purging daily when she came to the Eating Disorders Recovery Center. In treatment, she has been able to identify and express the anger and shame she feels toward her father for abandoning the family and the long-term effects this had on her self-concept.

"I think I'm beginning to let go of a lot of my history. I realize I can't change it. I don't feel as dirty as I used to or feel that my life is over and that this is all I have to show for it. I know my history doesn't control me as much as it used to because I've shared it so much and nobody's died from hearing it.

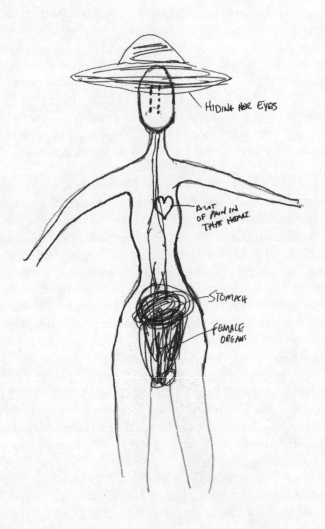

Figure 24. Sonni's Shame

"I continue to heal my shame by stopping and listening to my body when feelings emerge. The greatest thing I can do for myself is to continue to live one day at a time and be consciously aware of physical, emotional and spiritual recovery. One gift I can give myself is that, no matter where I am or what environment I'm surrounded by, I can live life to the fullest and celebrate life, not wallow in the shame that might once have almost strangled me."

For Faye, a compulsive overeater who is overweight and the survivor of an incestuous relationship with her father that lasted until she was about 10 years old, her statement and depiction of how she feels and perceives her body is simply, "My body doesn't exist." (See Fig. 25.) Faye has a dual shame regarding the incestuous relationship with her father. On one hand, she sees it as immoral and feels she has been in some way broken and made unworthy before God. Yet she also feels shame because she missed her father's attention and touching, once the incest stopped. It has been difficult for her to accept that every child craves physical contact and that it would only be natural to miss her father's touch and attention. The fact that she misses the touching that occurred through the incest is not a sign of moral depravity but a natural response to losing the only form of attention she ever received from her father.

In Faye's case, there was never any hugging, holding, patting, etc., other than during this incestuous interaction with her father.

Faye has blamed herself and her body for years as the cause for the incest and as the reason the relationship stopped. Her father's withdrawal from her and the family's denial that the sexual abuse ever occurred left her feeling bad and broken. It was hard for Faye to develop a less demeaning, less shaming attitude toward herself and her body because of the blame she has assumed for so many years. It has also been hard to allow herself to reach out for support and friendship from others because her fear of being exposed and then abandoned again is very intense.

Figure 25. Faye's Shame

Summary

In these personal stories, drawings and reflections, we and our patients have attempted to share concrete examples of how idealization promotes both bodyshame and selfshame in the individual with an eating disorder. Idealization is a by-product of any hierarchical system. Its purpose is, essentially, to keep the system intact by establishing certain physical and emotional qualities and characteristics as superior and the rest as inferior. This process keeps everyone in the system striving to be those things which have been defined as superior *whether or not this is who they want to be or feel instinctively inclined to be.* The motivation to override the internal and strive for what is defined as superior is the basic human desire that we all have to feel connected to the rest of humanity. The fear that this connection will be severed because we are different, unlike others, is intense because it is affiliated with our survival instinct.

As infants and children, we need the bonds to provide us with the basic survival needs of food and shelter, as well as basic emotional needs like mirroring, modeling, nurturing and learning how to nurture. As adults, though we may become physically capable of providing for our own physical survival needs, we do not outgrow our continuing emotional needs. Though the dynamics of our emotional needs will change as we grow and develop, the basic need for human affiliation remains the same throughout our lifetime.

In recovery, individuals with eating disorders need to learn to let go of idealization as a means of dismantling the selfshame and bodyshame that has perpetuated their disease. Dismantling shame begins with understanding what shame is and then uncovering how the shame has entangled itself into self-perceptions, body perceptions and ways of interpersonal relating.

In the next chapter, we will be sharing some of the methods of dismantling bodyshame and selfshame that many of our patients have found useful. But, as has been cited in the stories and reflections in this chapter, much of the dismantling of shame comes from the process of sharing the shame with others. It is through this process that shame loses its power. By releasing shame as *the secret*, we actually begin to experience the humanness of our imperfections and to recognize that being human does not mean we are destined to be alone.

6

Recovery

The Shame Of The Body

Given our dualistic, hierarchical mode of thinking, it is difficult to see ourselves as much more than a mind and a body. But if we are to develop a more loving relationship with our body and our spirit, we must conceive of ourselves as a living process, a process that is whole and cohesive, fluid and flexible, involving our body, our mind and our spirit.

We get into trouble when we maintain a static image of ourselves or when we are blinded by an ideal image upon which we become fixated, hypnotized. It is through the acceptance of these images as real that we start to use our bodies to help us achieve what we think is good and acceptable, to say to the world, "**I am good enough**."

When we lose ourselves as a living process, we become vulnerable to shame. As a living process, we develop a patient and accepting relationship with our body and our feelings. Our body is no longer an object to be starved, overfed, made-up, carved or decorated but rather an invaluable part of our whole.

Our wholeness encompasses the interrelationships between our masculine and feminine sides, our inner self and our body. Nothing is viewed as weaker or stronger, since each aspect takes and gives strength to the other.

Learning To Let Go And Empower Yourself

There are several steps to developing a more empathic, accepting relationship with your body and accepting the complementary relationship between your masculine and feminine sides so they can co-exist in a healthy way. Let's first examine some strategies for healing the shame that your body has absorbed.

Deep Breathing

Breathing is the first step in making a connection with your body. Most of our patients have great difficulty in following what appears to be a simple exercise in deep breathing. However, being alone with oneself and one's body requires basically that we like ourselves. Given the shame-based self-identity and body that we have grown to be self-conscious of and uncomfortable with — even to loathe — it is a very hard task, then, to simply be with ourselves, alone, exposed to ourselves, body and soul.

We ask our patients to spend only five minutes daily during the first week, doing the following deep breathing exercises. Increase the time according to your ability to succeed but try to stretch yourself and increase your alone-time weekly by five minutes, until you can comfortably reach 30 minutes of alone-time.

The purpose of deep breathing is to help you relax and to feel your body as a living, breathing process.

Directions:
1. Choose a quiet, comfortable spot where you will not be disturbed. Lie on the floor and breathe slowly, quietly. Anchor your attention to your breath.
2. Place one hand palm down over your navel and the other over it. Take a deep breath in through your nose. Feel your belly expand like a balloon filling with air.
3. As you exhale deeply through your mouth, gently push your abdomen in with your palm, squeezing out any remaining air.
4. Continue breathing this way, slowly and without forcing yourself in any way. Breathe deeply in through your nose and feel your belly expand. Imagine a balloon filling with air. As you exhale, gently push your abdomen with your palm, squeezing out any remaining air like a sigh of relief.
5. Do this for five minutes at your own pace, slowly, rhythmically, evenly. Let yourself feel the air as it rushes through your nose and into your lungs. Even though you may have difficulty keeping your mind uncluttered, anchor your attention to your breathing only. Be patient.

Most of our patients find it difficult to maintain concentration on their breath and breathing. Our mind wants to keep us distracted, either with tasks or with the uncomfortable, self-conscious feelings we have about being alone with our self and our body. Have faith and be patient.

Body-talk/Self-talk

Changing The Tapes

In trying to like our bodies and our whole inner self, the first thing we must do is to change our self-talk. Self-talk is something that everyone does. It is not an indication of anything being wrong! Self-talk is a major factor in how we feel about ourselves and our bodies. Self-talk can be defined as the tapes or messages that we tend to play over and over and over again in our heads. These tapes or messages are generally the ones we received from significant others, especially our parents. If we had loving, affirming parents, our tapes or self-talk tend to be positive. If, however, we had dysfunctional, critical, judgmental parents, our tapes replay accordingly. Self-talk centers around more than just our inner selves; for compulsive eaters it tends to focus on the body and defective body parts. Reframing or consciously altering our self-talk is a vital recovery tool but before we can reframe, we must first discover how destructive our self-talk and body-talk actually is.

Follow your thoughts for one or two days. Be vigilant in hearing the types of messages that you repeat about the qualities of your self and your body. These messages are often like a broken record — once having found a comfortable groove, they just keep playing over and over again. It might be a good idea if you carried a little notebook around and jotted down the major themes of your inner tapes, be they negative or positive. Pay particular attention to whether the self-talk is directed to your self as a person — "Boy, are you dumb! Why didn't you think of that first?" or to your body — "God! You have the fattest ass ever."

Given our experience, the positive messages are few and far between whereas the negative self-talk runs rampant. Our goal is to increase your positive self-messages and decrease the negative ones.

At the end of a few days, list which parts of your self, your personality, you tend to demean. Which of these are stereotypically female qualities?

Which parts of your body do you tend to demean?

Use the Body Esteem Checklist (see Appendix I) and the Masculine/Feminine Trait Checklist (see Appendix II) to help you evaluate your masculine/feminine predispositions.

Most of our self-talk messages revolve around the following:

Devaluing, negative beliefs about the self: Bette says, "I'm so damned fat! I can't stand it. Look at these arms, the flab hangs down to my knees but not far enough. You can still see how fat and dimpled my knees are. God, I'll never find a dress that will fit me. I'm just not going to go to the wedding. Nobody would miss me anyway."

The basis of this self-talk message is denigrating to both Bette's self-esteem and to her body-esteem. Much of our self-talk is based on messages we received from our parents, teachers or significant others. Even though we received these messages as children, as adults we never think to challenge them and refuse to accept them.

After maintaining a diary of your self-talk and body-talk themes, indicate where you think you picked up the messages — from a parent, a teacher, a friend? Start to challenge the basis of these messages and replace them with more self-affirming messages.

Shoulds, oughts and if onlys — cultural expectations and standards: As you increase your self-talk awareness, pay close attention to your shoulds, oughts and if onlys. We tend to have a set of standards by which we operate and we believe that if we measured up to them, life would be grand. For example, a common *should* for compulsive eaters is *I shouldn't have eaten that cookie . . . If only I were thinner, I would have got that job . . . I shouldn't feel this way.* These are traps that need investigating and challenging.

Shoulds imply perfectionism and generally cast blame on others. They are dangerous self-talk words that perpetuate a continual division within the self and between the self and the body.

Denigrating and disaster-planning: Another self-talk trap is to denigrate oneself and disaster - plan. *If I don't lose weight before the wedding, everyone will think I have no will power. They'll all laugh at me behind my back and say, "Poor Judy, always a bridesmaid never a bride. She's so fat, who would ever want to marry her?"* Thinking of the worst possible outcome and all the worst possible details will perpetuate a negative relationship with yourself and your body. Self-denigraters dwell not only on what could happen in the future but also stay focused on the past and berate themselves constantly for not being perfect. *I really screwed up when I gave* *that presentation. I didn't know the answer to that guy's question. They all must think I'm really stupid. I noticed one woman staring at my legs. I know she was thinking how fat and misshapen they are. God, I'm such a failure.*

You can see how this message might lead a person to feel really bad about herself! Now is the time to replace your negative messages with positive ones. Let's go back to our previous example. *I did a good job on the presentation. Even though I didn't know the answer to that question, I handled myself well. I can't know the answer to every question someone might ask. After all, I'm only human.*

Make a list of what you like most about yourself, physically, and otherwise. Which of your physical attributes do you like best? Hair? Color of eyes? Skin? Develop a list of positive affirmations so you can replace your old, critical tapes with what you do like about yourself.

If it's difficult to come up with some physical and personal qualities that you like, ask a few good friends or your support group members to help you. However, you are not allowed to challenge or question what they perceive as a physical asset or personal strength. You are simply to say *thank you* and write them in your notebook of affirmations.

Reframing

Reframing can only happen when you realize that the frame of reference you have been using is not productive or self-affirming. If you really believe you are unattractive and always will be, then you are hopeless. However, if you are willing to reframe this belief about yourself, you can begin a healing relationship with your self and your body.

Affirmations challenge our old, self-destructive tapes by continually eroding our old, ingrained self-messages and substituting new messages that change our frame of reference. Affirmations help us to reprogram our unconscious. In developing your affirmations, you must phrase them in the positive; never use the word *not* in your affirmations. For example, *I will not binge,* is not an affirmation. *I will eat healthy foods today,* or *I have a healthy relationship with food,* are affirming.

Develop some affirmations that focus on your attitude about your body: *I like my body when I am eating in a healthy fashion . . . I have attractive legs . . . I have nice arms.*

Many of our patients are uncomfortable at first with these affirmations. They think they are lying to themselves if they say they like parts of their body which they actually believe are unacceptable . . .Well, it is not deceptive to be kind, loving and affirming toward yourself.

Remember, your standard for what your body *should* look like is highly influenced by our culture. Free yourself from this trap by at least affirming yourself. Our patients report feeling embarrassed with this assignment. We remind them: No one else can hear you. You are the only person listening to what you are saying. What have you got to lose?

Bodyscan And Affirmations

Exercise 1: Following the directions for deep breathing, get yourself very relaxed on the floor. Once you feel relaxed, do the following.

Starting with your toes, focus your attention on those body parts. Spend 10 to 20 seconds engaging in positive thoughts about your toes. For example, *I have nice soft toes. They are cute and cuddly.* Continue this with each body part: feet, ankles, calves, knees, thighs, abdomen, buttocks, hips, breasts, fingers, hands, forearms, shoulders, neck, face, head, skin.

This will not be an easy task at first. The difficulty is commensurate with the intensity of your bodyloathing. The purpose is to get you to develop an affirming, positive relationship with your body rather than a degrading punitive one.

Exercise 2: Sit quietly and relax. Close your eyes and bring to mind the part of your body that you most dislike or neglect. Allow yourself to sit quietly and simply experience this part of yourself. Speak to it as you usually do, expressing all your feelings. Listen to your body part's response. What is it saying back to you? How do you feel? How does it feel?

Ask this body part what it needs from you, how it wants to be loved and cared for by you. Dialogue with it. Write your feelings about the dialogue in your journal and commit to implementing your body part's request for care and nurturance.

Mother/Daughter Bodies

Since mothers play a vital role in our psychological development as well as our physical development, it would be helpful to determine how much of your body image is based on your mother's body.

Reflect for a few minutes on what messages you heard your mother speak regarding her body. Write these down in your notebook.

Using the Body Esteem Checklist, indicate how you think your mother would have answered each item. How similar is this to your own feelings about your body?

What specific messages did your mother give you regarding your body? Write these down in your notebook.

Once you have gathered this data, sit back and reflect on whose body image you really have? Write down your thoughts in your journal.

Shame/Pride/Joy Exercise

For this exercise you need three pieces of paper. On the first, draw a circle in the center of the page. Write the word SHAME in its center. Then all around the circle, write those things you are ashamed of.

On the second sheet, draw a circle in the center of the page. This time, write the word PROUD in the center. Now write all the things you feel proud of around the circle.

On the third sheet, after drawing a circle in the center of the page, write JOY in the center. Around this circle, write all the things that bring you joy.

Now look at all three circles. It is not unusual for shame-based individuals to have many more things listed around shame than the other two. This is because the shame-based person's energy and attention are focused more on those things which promote shame than on those which promote healthy pride and joy.

It is a very healing experience to commit to giving daily attention to your pride and joy circles. Also, develop a plan to enhance joy in your life by doing or spending time with at least one of the items around your joy circle at least once weekly.

After 30 days of reflecting and participating in joyful and healthy pride-inducing experiences, think about any changes in the level of your stress, anger, isolation, shame. Then commit yourself to enhancing joy and healthy pride for another 30 days.

Visualization

We all carry a visual image or picture of our bodies in our imagination. If the image is negative or distorted, it perpetuates a negative body image and promotes feelings of self-hate. Visualization is a process which allows us not only to use our imagination in promoting a more positive body image but it can also be used to change attitudes and beliefs about our inner selves.

Visualizations always begin with a relaxation exercise so that you can be fully receptive to the new images you will be creating.

Progressive Relaxation Exercise

Sit upright in a comfortable chair. Slowly, do your deep breathing, being sure to take at least five slow, deep breaths.

Quietly attend to your body parts and as you do, remember that with every outgoing breath, each body part will become more and more relaxed.

Attend to your toes and feet. With every outgoing breath, they become more and more relaxed.

Attend to your calves. With every outgoing breath, they become more and more relaxed.

Attend to your knees and thighs. With every outgoing breath they become more and more relaxed.

Attend to your hips and lower back. With every outgoing breath, they become more and more relaxed.

Attend to your buttocks. With every outgoing breath, they become more and more relaxed.

You are beginning to feel numb. You feel as if you are floating.

Attend to your abdomen. With every outgoing breath, it becomes more and more relaxed.

Attend to your fingers and hands. With every outgoing breath, they become more and more relaxed.

Attend to your arms. With every outgoing breath, they become more and more relaxed.

Attend to your shoulders. With every outgoing breath, they become more and more relaxed.

Attend to your neck. With every outgoing breath, it becomes more and more relaxed.

Attend to your jaws and tongue. With every outgoing breath, they become more and more relaxed.

Attend to your forehead and eyes. With every outgoing breath, they become more and more relaxed.

Scan your body for any signs of tension. With every outgoing breath the tension will disappear.

Your entire body is now fully relaxed.

Exercise 1: Once you have completed the progressive relaxation exercise and you feel as though you are floating, surround yourself with peace and calm. Feel a warm, subtle glow surrounding you. Imagine yourself standing in this glow. See a person approaching you. This person bears with him or her a shaming message. Recognize the person's face. Listen to the person's message. Notice that the glow protects you from the shaming message. Tell the person, *You are powerless against the light.*

See the person turn and leave, taking the shaming message away. Allow the glow around you to penetrate your skin, healing and soothing you.

Exercise 2: Sit quietly. Imagine shame filling your body, washing over you. Think of shame-producing events, words, situations. Just allow that shame to flow over your body. Feel it on your skin. Now take a deep breath. Imagine a cloud floating overhead, magical and shining. Look up at it, noticing a gently sparkling rain beginning to fall from it. Feel the rain caressing your face, your arms, your chest, your entire body, with a healing and tingling sensation. Feel the shame being washed away, leaving behind a feeling of peace and renewal. With your hands, feel your skin. You are cleansed. Say to yourself, *I am whole and at peace.*

Exercise 3: Visualize your feminine self. Give your feminine self a form and shape. It can be an object, having any shape, form or color, any texture, smell, sound. Become aware of how you feel about your feminine side. If you have any negative response to your feminine side, allow the feelings, with every breath you take, to be replaced with feelings of receptivity and openness. If you have any positive responses to your feminine side, allow yourself to fully enjoy these good feelings.

Talk to the symbol of your feminine side. What do you like about it? What does it like about you? Ask your feminine side what it needs from you to feel affirmed and valued.

Tell your feminine side what you believe its strengths are. Tell your feminine side what you believe its weaknesses are. Continue to affirm your feminine side by repeating the following affirmation. *I feel warm and loving toward you. You are an important part of my total self. I appreciate the qualities you give me.*

Now visualize your masculine self. Again, it can be any object, having any shape, form or color, any texture, smell or sound. Give form and shape to your masculine side. Become aware of how you feel about your masculine side. If you have any negative responses toward your masculine side, allow them to be replaced, with every breath you take, with feelings of receptivity and openness. If you have any positive response to your masculine side, allow yourself to enjoy these good feelings.

Talk to the symbol of your masculine side. What do you like about it? What does it like about you? Ask your masculine side what it needs from you to feel valued and affirmed. Tell your masculine side what you believe to be its strengths. Tell your masculine side what you believe to be its weaknesses. Continue affirming your masculine side by repeating the following affirmation. *I feel warm and loving toward you. You are an important part of my total self. I appreciate the qualities you give me.*

Now visualize your masculine and feminine symbols in concert with each other. Feel the inner strength when they come together. Allow yourself to be open to an inner sense of cooperation, harmony and joy as they complement each other.

Try to spend at least 15 minutes every day with your masculine/feminine sides.

Exercise 4: This exercise focuses on developing an awareness of and affirmation of your Inner Child.

After relaxing, open your mind's eye to a scene. Imagine yourself standing in a beautiful park. It is a gorgeous sunny day. Allow yourself to feel the warmth of the sun's rays on your back and shoulders. You can feel a warm summer breeze gently brushing against your cheek. You can hear all the sounds of the park, the birds singing, the children laughing, the squirrels scurrying about. You are standing on a path. Begin slowly to walk down the path, enjoying the scenery around you. As you walk along, you see in the distance ahead a small figure sitting on a park bench. Allow yourself to continue along the path. As you draw nearer, you recognize that the figure on the bench is a child. Then you realize that the child sitting on the bench is you — as a child. Stop for a few moments and pay attention to how you are feeling as you see yourself, a child, in front of you.

Continue to walk toward the child. When you reach the bench, sit down as near or as far away from the child as is comfortable for you. Again, take time to notice your feelings.

Now look into the face of the child. What do you see in this face? The child is also looking at you. If there is anything you would like to say to the child at this time, do so. Allow the child to say anything to you that she needs to say. Pick the child up and place her on your lap. Wrap your arms around her and give her a big hug. Simply sit quietly for a time with your arms around the child. Feel her head against your shoulder, her hair brushing against your cheek. Allow yourself to just sit together with the child for a time.

After a while it is time to leave this place. Now that you have made contact with your child, remember that you can take her with you wherever you go. She will always be with you. Once again, focus your attention on your deep breathing. As you continue to breathe, slowly close your mind to the scene of yourself and the child sitting together on the park bench.

Take time to write in your journal what this experience was like for you. What feelings did you have when you first recognized that it was you, as a child, sitting on the park bench? How did you feel when you sat down with the child? What did you see in the child's face? What did you need to say to the child? What did the child need to say to you? How did it feel to embrace the child on your lap?

Some individuals experience great love and joy in renewing their relationship with their Inner Child. Others feel fear, anger or sadness. If you felt love and joy, you may want to give yourself the opportunity to communicate with your Inner Child on a daily basis. This can bring a greater sense of self-acceptance and affirmation. If, however, your feelings in response to being with your Inner Child were painful, you need to explore where these feelings come from. Often they are coverups for shame which you absorbed as a child and continue to carry.

Your ongoing visualizations could focus on the shame that the child feels. You, now an adult, can help and nurture the Inner Child to dismantle her unhealthy shame by spending time with her and communicating and affirming her basic goodness.

Don't limit yourself to these visualizations. Try to be as creative as you can in developing your own visualizations.

Family Shame

Shamegram

In order to fully appreciate the transmission of generational shame themes and to help you distinguish your own shame from your family's shame, complete a Shamegram. If you can interview your family members, it will be helpful. If not, you can still complete the Shamegram, given what you know about each person.

A Shamegram is initially very similar to a genogram. A genogram is a method of visually depicting how a family has structured itself. It's like a map which can show how a family operates. When a genogram is completed, especially if it includes more than one generation of a family, it can visually demonstrate any family rules, family roles or patterns of interaction that have been passed on from one generation to the next.

Begin by depicting your family of origin on paper. If you can go back one or more generations, your learning experience will be enhanced. However, it is not essential. You may use any symbol for each family member that you wish — squares, triangles, pictures. Place these symbols on the paper in a way that represents how it felt to grow up in your family. For example, if your father was the dominating, central figure of the family, his symbol might be larger than the others and in the center of the page. If you saw your brother as always removed from the family in some way, his symbol might be off to the side, distanced from the others.

Once you have each individual's symbol positioned on the page, draw lines and arrows between the symbols which signify the communication patterns within the family. For example, a solid line with arrows facing both ways might depict open communication. A bold, jagged line with one arrow might represent angry one-way communication.

Next comes color-coding. For each individual, color in all or part of the symbol to represent this person's life experiences. Focus on chronic illness such as alcoholism, eating disorders, cancer, diabetes, heart disease, etc. Also, include significant losses such as miscarriages, divorces, premature death of parents and any other life experiences you believe may have had an impact on this individual's attitudes and openness to communicate with others.

Once you have completed your drawing, write down all the memories and descriptions you can about each individual and about the family as a whole. Ask yourself what each individual may have felt shame about. Ask yourself what the family as a whole may have been ashamed of. Then reflect on how similar or dissimilar your own shame feelings are to the shame of other family members and the family as a whole.

Write your reflections and impressions in your journal and think about how much of the shame you experience truly belongs to you and how much you absorbed from others.

As this becomes clear to you, affirm yourself and your conclusions by saying: *This shame* [name it] *belongs to* _____, *not to me. I no longer need to carry this shame as my own.* You may want to repeat this affirmation daily for a time to help you become more comfortable with letting go of the shame.

In this chapter we have offered a few exercises designed not only to help in identifying shame but also in focusing on the healing of selfshame and bodyshame.

There are other resources and additional exercises and activities to help individuals to dismantle selfshame and provide help in feeling more centered and accepting of the physical body. Participating in yoga, seeking the assistance of a massage therapist or participating in art therapy or dance therapy can also be very useful.

The most important element of such exercises is that they allow for the integration of the mind, body and spirit. When this integration is nurtured, embracing both the feminine and masculine aspects of the self comes naturally. The renewed sense of internal wholeness allows the individual to develop wholeness in her interpersonal relationships and in relationship with the Higher Power.

Summary

 Addiction prevents the actual development of the authentic or real self. Whatever the focus of the addiction, whether it be food and thinness, alcohol or achievement, the individual struggling with the addiction is imprisoned by deep feelings of personal shame.

For the person who has an eating disorder, this shame is experienced on two levels: selfshame — feelings of personal inferiority — and bodyshame — feelings of physical inferiority. Our culture continues to foster this dual shame bind by its overvaluing of the masculine and its devaluing of the feminine.

Individuals who suffer from an eating disorder are acting out the conflict that we all experience in trying to heal the split between our masculine and feminine sides, between ourselves, nature and God. Much like the individual who acts out the symptoms of the dysfunctional family, the person with an eating disorder acts out the dysfunction of the hierarchical culture. Much like the individual who is identified as a "problem" or a troubled person, the eating disordered individual is often viewed as weak willed, disgusting and out of control. Much like the troubled individual who is, in fact, absorbing the pain and conflicts of the family, the eating disordered individual absorbs the pain and conflicts of a culture that cannot even recognize the split between its masculine and feminine sides. And much like the troubled individual who feels desperately alone and misunderstood, the eating disordered individual experiences deep feelings of isolation and alienation.

In order for healing to begin, the dysfunctional family must learn to take responsibility for and recognize its conflicts in order for all of its members to develop to their full potential as human beings. Likewise, our culture must also learn to take responsibility for and recognize its onesidedness in order for all of its members to develop their full potential.

The inner emptiness experienced by the person with an eating disorder can never be healed by food, by having the ideal body or through a string of accomplishments. This hole can only be healed through self-acceptance. Such self-acceptance must include being able to accept our human strengths and frailties. It must also include breaking away from the hierarchical culture's pattern of overvaluing control, a *power-over* mentality, and independence at the expense of the useful skills and the basic human need for cooperation, nurturance and affiliation.

It is when, as individuals and as a culture, we can practice a life of blending decision-making with cooperative effort, when we can value the process necessary to achieve a goal as much as the goal itself, that the collective shame experience can be dismantled. As the collective shame diminishes, each individual within our culture will experience the freedom to embrace the masculine and feminine aspects without fear of rejection or recrimination by others.

Although addiction is insidious, we also need to appreciate what it can teach us . . . that we are simply human beings fraught with conflicts, physical and personal imperfections and limitations. Addiction also attempts to show all of us that if we try to live life in a one-sided way — if we embrace only the masculine aspects of life — we are doomed to living a life of vacillating extremes and a constant searching for the missing piece we feel but cannot necessarily see.

The recovery process often becomes the pathway through which an individual can give birth to a whole, authentic self which encompasses an equal appreciation and comfort with both the masculine and feminine sides. This relieves the inner emptiness and allows the recovering individual to experience serenity by feeling connected with herself, with others and with a Higher Power.

Chapter Notes

Chapter 1

(1) Wurmser, Leon. **The Mask of Shame.** pp. 43-45. Baltimore: Johns Hopkins University Press, 1982.

(2) Kurtz, Ernie. **Shame and Guilt: Characteristics of the Dependency Cycle.** Center City, MN: Hazelden, 1981.

(3) Bradshaw, John. **Healing The Shame That Binds You.** Deerfield Beach, FL: Health Communications, 1988.

(4) Schneider, Carl. "A Mature Sense of Shame," in Nathanson, Donald. **The Many Faces of Shame.** New York: Guilford Press, 1987.

(5) Horney, Karen. **Neurosis and Human Growth.** New York: Norton, 1950.

(6) Kurtz, Ernie. **Shame and Guilt.**

(7) Wurmser, Leon. **The Mask of Shame.**

(8) Lynd, Helen Merrell. **On Shame And The Search For Identity.** New York: Harcourt, Brace, 1958.

(9) Nathanson, Donald. "The Shame/Pride Axis," in Lewis, Helen Block, Ed. **The Role of Shame in Symptom Formation.** New York: Laurence Baum, 1987.

(10) Nathanson, Donald. "The Shame/Pride Axis," p. 191.

Chapter 2

(1) Miller, Susan. **The Shame Experience.** London: Lawrence Erblaum, 1985.

(2) Ibid.

(3) Ibid.

(4) Ibid.

(5) Ibid.

(6) Ibid.

(7) Ibid.

(8) Ibid.

(9) Kaufman, Gershen. **Shame: The Power Of Caring.** Cambridge, MA: Schenkman Books, 1985.

(10) Ibid. Chaper One.

(11) Kaufman, Gershen. "The meaning of shame: toward a self-affirming identity," in *Journal of Counseling Psychology,* Volume 21, No. 6, pp. 568-574, 1974.

(12) _____. **Shame: The Power Of Caring,** Chapter Two.

(13) Ibid, p. 35.

(14) Reference to Tomkins, Silvan can be found in: Izard, Carroll. **Human Emotions.** New York: Plenum Press, 1977.

(15) Nathanson, Donald. "A Timetable for Shame" in Nathanson, Donald, Ed., **The Many Faces Of Shame.** New York: Guilford Press, 1987.

(16) Surrey, Janet. *"Self-in-relation: A theory of women's development,"* in work in progress. Wellesley, MA: Stone Center for Developmental Services and Studies, Wellesley College, 1985.

(17) Gilligan, Carol. **In A Different Voice: Psychological Theory and Women's Development,** p. 6. Cambridge, MA: Harvard University Press, 1982.

(18) Chodorow, Nancy, as discussed in Gilligan, Carol. **In A Different Voice.**

(19) Gilligan, **In A Different Voice,** p. 8.

(20) Surrey, Janet, *Self-in-relation,* p. 6.

(21) Ibid, p. 8.

(22) Kohut, Heinz. **Analysis of the Self.** New York: International University Press, 1971.

(23) McFarland, B. and Baumann, T. **Feeding The Empty Heart.** New York: Harper/Hazelden, 1987.

(24) Chernin, Kim. **The Obsession: Reflections on the Tyranny of Slenderness.** New York: Harper & Row, 1982.

Chapter 3

(1) **Webster's Ninth New Collegiate Dictionary.** Springfield, MA: Merriam-Webster, 1987.

(2) Campbell, Joseph. **The Power of Myth with Bill Moyers.** New York: Doubleday, 1988.

(3) Eisler, Riane. **The Chalice and the Blade.** San Francisco: Harper & Row, 1987.

(4) Watts, Alan W. **Nature, Man and Woman.** New York: Vantage Books, 1970.

(5) Ochs, Carol. **Behind the Sex of God.** Boston: Beacon Press, 1977.

(6) Watts, **Nature, Man and Woman,** p. 3.

(7) Turner, Bryan, S. **The Body and Society.** New York: Blackwell, 1984.

(8) Banner, Lois. **American Beauty.** New York: Alfred A. Knopf, 1983.

(9) Freedman, Rita. **Beauty Bound.** Lexington, MA: DC Heath, 1986.

(10) Ibid, p. 18.

(11) Ibid. p. 20.

(12) Banner, **American Beauty,** p. 13.

(13) Ibid, p. 14.

(14) Ibid, p. 5.

(15) Freedman, **Beauty Bound,** p. 223.

(16) Corliss, Richard. "The New Ideal of Beauty," in *Time,* August 20, 1982.

(17) Ehrenreich, Barbara and English, Deirdre. **For Her Own Good.** New York: Anchor Press, 1979.

(18) Banner, **American Beauty,** p. 72.

(19) Brumberg, Joan. **Fasting Girls: The Emergence Of Anorexia Nervosa As A Modern Disease.** Cambridge, MA: Harvard University Press, 1988.

(20) Peters, LuLu Hunt. **Diet and Health with a Key to the Calories.** Chicago: Reilly & Lee, 1918.

(21) Root, Maria, Fallon, P. and Friedrich, Wm. **Bulimia: A Systems Approach to Treatment.** New York: Norton, 1986.

(22) Striegel-Moore, R., Silberstein, L. and Rodin, J. "Toward an understanding of risk factors for bulimia," in *American Psychologist,* Vol. 41, No. 3, March, 1986.

(23) "American Beauty" in *American Health Magazine,* July/August, 1988.

(24) Hamburger, Annette. "Beauty Quest" in *Psychology Today.* May, 1988, pp. 28-32.

(25) Freedman, **Beauty Bound,** p. 151.

(26) Woodman, Marion. "Addiction to Perfection" in *Yoga Journal,* November/December, 1988.

(27) Orbach, Susie. **The Hunger Strike.** New York: Norton, 1986.

Chapter 4

(1) Lerner, R.M., Karabenick, S.A. and Stuart, J.L. "Relations among physical attractiveness, body attitudes and self-concept in male and female college students" in *Journal of Psychology,* Vol. 85, pp. 119-129. 1973.
Secord, P.F. and Jourard, S.M. "The appraisal of body-cathexis: Body-cathexis and the self" in *Journal of Consulting Psychology,* Vol. 17, pp. 343-347. 1953.

(2) Powers, Pamela and Erickson, Marilyn. "Body image in women and its relationship to self-image and body satisfaction" in *The Journal of Obesity & Weight Regulation,* 5, Spring, 1986, pp. 37-50.

(3) Lugo, James and Hershey, Gerald. **Human Development.** New York: Macmillan, 1974, pp. 125-127.

(4) Ibid, p. 276.

(5) Garner, D.M. and Garfinkel, P.E. "Body image in anorexia nervosa: measurement, theory and clinical implications" in *International Journal of Psychiatry in Medicine,* 11, 1981, p. 263-284.

(6) Shilder, P. **The Image and Appearance of the Human Body.** New York: International University Press, 1950.

(7) Kearney-Cook, Ann. "Decoding the obsession: using

guided imagery in the treatment of body image disturbance among bulimic women" from draft of chapter prepared for Hornyak, L. and Baker, E., **Handbook of Experiential Techniques in the Treatment of Eating Disorders.**

(8) Fisher, S. **Development and Structure of Body Image**. Hillsdale, NJ: Erlbaum, 1986.

(9) Mahler, M., Pine, F. and Bergman, A. **The Psychological Birth of the Human Infant**. New York: Norton, 1975.

(10) Tronick, E., Als, H., Adamson, L., Wise, S. and Brazelton, T. "The infant's response to entrapment between contradictory messages in face-to-face interaction" *Journal of Child Psychiatry*, Vol. 17, 1978, pp. 1-13.

(11) Rubin, J., Provenzano, F. and Luria, Z. "The eye of the beholder: Parents' views on sex of newborns" in *American Journal of Orthopsychiatry*, Vol. 44, 1974, pp. 512-519.

(12) Henschel-Ambert, A.M. **Sex Structure**. Don Mills, Ont: Longman Canada, 1973.

(13) Broverman, I., Broverman, D., Clarkson, F., Rosencrantz, P. and Vogel, S. "Sex role stereotypes and clinical judgments of mental health" in *Journal of Consulting and Clinical Psychology*, 34, 1970, pp. 1-7.

(14) Striegel-Moore, R., Silberstein, L. and Rodin, J. "Toward an understanding of risk factors for bulimia" in *American Psychologist*, 41, 1986, pp. 246-263.

(15) Crisp, A.H. and Kalucy, R.S. "Aspects of the perceptual disorder in anorexia females" in *Journal of Psychopathology and Behavioral Assessment*, 7, 1974, pp. 289-301.
Rosenbaum, M. "The changing body image of the adolescent girl" in Sugar, M. Ed., **Female Adolescent Development**, New York: Brunner/Mazel, 1979, pp. 234-252.

(16) Dweck, C., Davidson, W., Nelson, S., Bradley, E. "Sex differences in learned helplessness: II The contingencies of evaluative feedback in the classroom and III: An experimental analysis" in *Developmental Psychology*. Vol. 14 (3), May, 1978, pp. 268-276.

(17) Chodorow, N. **The Reproduction of Mothering: Psychoanalysis and the Sociology of Gender.** Berkeley: University of California Press, 1978.

(18) Simmons, R.G. and Rosenberg, F. "Sex, sex roles and self-image" in *Journal of Youth and Adolescence*, 4, 1975, pp. 229-258.

(19) Douvan E. and Adelson, J. **The Adolescent Experience.** New York: Wiley, 1966.

(20) Gilligan, Carol. **In A Different Voice: Psychological Theory and Women's Development.** Cambridge, MA: Harvard University Press, 1982.

(21) Hood, J., Moore, T. and Garner, D. "Locus of control as a measure of ineffectiveness in anorexia nervosa" in *Journal of Consulting and Clinical Psychology,* Vol. 50 (1), 1982, pp. 3-13.

(22) Steele, C.I. "Weight loss among teenage girls: An adolescent crisis" in *Adolescence,* 15, 1980, pp. 823-829.

(23) Striegel-Moore, Ruth, Silberstein, Lisa and Rodin, Judith. "Toward an understanding of risk factors for bulimia" in *American Psychologist*, Vol. 41, no. 3, 1986, pp. 246-263.

(24) Kearney-Cook, Ann. "Group treatment of sexual abuse among women with eating disorders" in *Women and Therapy,* Fall, 1987.

(25) Bass, E. and Davis, L. **The Courage to Heal.** New York: Harper & Row, 1988.

(26) Goldenson, Robert, Ed. **Disability and Rehabilitation Handbook.** New York: McGraw-Hill, 1978.

(27) Lugo and Hershey, **Human Development**, 1974.

Appendix I

Body Esteem Checklist

To increase your awareness of your bodyshame, please rate each of the listed body parts or body processes below, using the following scale:

1 = strongly like   4 = dislike
2 = like   5 = strongly dislike
3 = neutral

head ___	hair ___	ears ___
neck ___	face ___	skin ___
nose ___	eyes ___	lips ___
teeth ___	smile ___	shoulders ___
back ___	chest/breasts ___	waist ___
hips ___	buttocks ___	penis/vagina ___
upper arms ___	forearms ___	wrists ___
hands ___	fingers ___	fingernails ___
thighs ___	knees ___	calves ___
ankles ___	feet ___	toes ___
appetite ___	body build ___	body hair ___
body scent ___	energy level ___	menstruation ___
sex drive ___	weight ___	

Circle all of the items you rated 4 or 5. Refer to the Body-talk/Self-talk exercise in chapter 6 to help you develop more positive feelings about all your body's parts and processes.

Appendix II

Masculine/Feminine Trait Checklist

To increase awareness of your feelings regarding your masculine/feminine sides, please rate each of the listed traits below, using the following scale:

1 = strongly like me   4 = unlike me
2 = like me   5 = strongly unlike me
3 = neutral

softspoken ____   **self-sufficient** ____

independent ____   *jealous* ____

warm ____   **competitive** ____

rational ____   *cooperative* ____

people-oriented ____   **athletic** ____

decisive ____   *creative* ____

compliant ____   **dominant** ____

aggressive ____   *sympathetic* ____

compassionate ____   **forceful** ____

success-oriented ____   *tactful* ____

child-oriented ____   **leadership abilities** ____

analytical ____   *gentle* ____

helpful ____   **self-reliant** ____

task-oriented ____   *moody* ____

tender ____   **forthright** ____

Now place a star next to the traits you identify with (rated 1 and 2) and of which you are proud.

Place a check mark next to the traits you identify with (rated 1 and 2) that you are ashamed of.

Next, notice all the italicized traits. The italicized traits are stereotypically feminine qualities. Take time to reflect on how you have rated yourself on these qualities. Did you indicate they are traits you feel proud of or ashamed of?

The bold traits are stereotypically masculine qualities. Take time to reflect on how you have rated yourself on these qualities. Did you indicate these are traits you feel proud of or ashamed of?

The Checklist is intended to help make you better aware of your biases regarding your masculine and feminine sides. Actually, the qualities themselves are neither good nor bad, strong nor weak. They are simply qualities that we each possess to a greater or lesser degree. Try not to assign value to any of the traits on the Checklist. Each quality is a strength except when it is extreme and rigidly manifested in every life situation. For example, compliance, in certain circumstances, is a strength. If it hinders healthy functioning or interrelating, however, it then is a liability because it greatly interferes with the individual's ability to appropriately stand up for herself.

Refer to the Visualization section in chapter 6 for an exercise designed to heal the conflicts around your masculine/feminine polarities.

Bibliography

"American Beauty" in *American Health Magazine*, July/August, 1988.

Banner, Lois. **American Beauty**. New York: Alfred A. Knopf, 1983.

Bass, Ellen and Davis, Linda. **The Courage to Heal**. New York: Harper and Row, 1988.

Bradshaw, John. **Healing The Shame That Binds You**. Deerfield Beach, FL: Health Communications, 1988.

Brumberg, Joan. **Fasting Girls: The Emergence Of Anorexia Nervosa As A Modern Disease**. Cambridge, MA: Harvard University Press, 1988.

Campbell, Joseph. **The Power of Myth with Bill Moyers**. New York: Doubleday, 1988.

Chernin, Kim. **The Obsession: Reflections on the Tyranny of Slenderness**. New York: Harper and Row, 1982.

——————. **The Hungry Self**. New York: Harper and Row, 1985.

Corliss, Richard. "The New Ideal of Beauty" in *Time*, August 20, 1982.

Ehrenreich, Barbara and English, Deirdre. **For Her Own Good**. New York: Anchor Press, 1979.

Eichenbaum, Louise and Orbach, Susie. **Understanding Women: a Feminist Psychoanalytic Approach**. New York: Basic Books, 1982.

Eisler, Riane. **The Chalice and the Blade**. New York: Harper and Row, 1982.

Freedman, Rita. **BodyLove**. New York: Harper and Row, 1988.

_____. **Beauty Bound**. Lexington, MA: D.C. Heath, 1986.

Garner, D.M., Garfinkel, P.E., Schwartz, D. and Thompson, M. "Cultural expectations of thinness in women" in *Psychological Reports*, vol. 47, Oct. 1980, pp. 483-491.

Gilligan, Carol. **In A Different Voice: Psychological Theory And Women's Development**. Cambridge: Harvard University Press, 1982.

Goldenson, Robert, Ed. **Disability and Rehabilitation Handbook**. New York: McGraw-Hill, 1978.

Hamburger, Annette. "Beauty Quest" in *Psychology Today*, 1988, pp. 28-32.

Horney, Karen. **Neurosis and Human Growth**. New York: Norton Press, 1950.

Izard, Carroll. **Human Emotions**. New York: Plenum Press, 1977.

Kaufman, Gershen. **Shame: The Power Of Caring**. Cambridge, MA: Schenkman Books, 1985.

_____. "The meaning of shame: toward a self-affirming identity" in *Journal of Counseling Psychology*, vol. 21, No. 6, 1974.

Kurtz, Ernie. **Shame and Guilt: Characteristics of the Dependency Cycle**. Center City, MN: Hazelden, 1981.

Lewis, Helen Block. "Shame and Guilt in Human Nature" in S. Tuttman, C. Kaye and M. Zimmerman, Eds., **Object And Self: A Developmental Approach**. New York: International Universities Press, 1981.

Lugo, James and Hershey, Gerald. **Human Development**. New York: Macmillan Publishing, 1974.

Lynd, Helen Merrell. **On Shame and The Search for Identity**. New York: Harcourt, Brace, 1958.

McFarland, B. and Baumann, T. **Feeding The Empty Heart**. New York: Harper/Hazelden, 1987.

Miller, Susan. **The Shame Experience**. Hillsdale, NJ: Lawrence Erlbaum, 1985.

_____. "The Shame/Pride Axis" as found in Lewis, Helen Block Lewis, Ed., **The Role of Shame in Symptom Formation**. New York: Laurence Baum, 1987.

Ochs, Carol. **Behind the Sex of God**. Boston: Beacon Press, 1977.

Orbach, Susie. **The Hunger Strike**. New York: Norton Press, 1986.

Peters, LuLu Hunt. **Diet and Health with a Key to the Calories**. Chicago: Reilly and Lee, 1918.

Piers, G. and Singer, M. **Shame and Guilt**. Springfield, IL: Thomas, 1953.

Root, Maria, Fallon, P. and Friedrich, Wm. **Bulimia: A Systems Approach to Treatment**. New York: Norton Press, 1986.

Sanford, Linda and Donovan, Mary Ellen. **Women and Self-Esteem: Understanding and Improving the Way We Think and Feel About Ourselves**. New York: Penguin, 1978.

Schneider, Carl. "A Mature Sense of Shame" in Nathanson, Donald, Ed. **The Many Faces of Shame**. New York: Guilford Press, 1987.

Striegel-Moore, R., Silberstein, L. and Rodin, J. "Toward an understanding of risk factors for bulimia" in *American Psychologist*, vol. 41, No. 3, 1986.

Turner, Bryan. **The Body and Society**. Oxford, England: Blackwell, 1984.

Watts, Alan. **Nature, Man and Woman**. New York: Vintage Books, 1970.

Woodman, Marion. "Addiction to Perfection" in *Yoga Journal*, November/December, 1988.

Wurmser, Leon. **The Mask of Shame**. Baltimore: Johns Hopkins University Press, 1981.

Books from . . .
Health Communications

AFTER THE TEARS: Reclaiming The Personal Losses of Childhood
Jane Middelton-Moz and Lorie Dwinell
Your lost childhood must be grieved in order for you to recapture your
self-worth and enjoyment of life. This book will show you how.
ISBN 0-932194-36-2 $7.95

HEALING YOUR SEXUAL SELF
Janet Woititz
How can you break through the aftermath of sexual abuse and enter into
healthy relationships? Survivors are shown how to recognize the problem
and deal effectively with it.
ISBN 1-55874-018-X $7.95

RECOVERY FROM RESCUING
Jacqueline Castine
Effective psychological and spiritual principles teach you when to take
charge, when to let go, and how to break the cycle of guilt and fear that
keeps you in the responsibility trap. Mind-altering ideas and exercises will
guide you to a more carefree life.
ISBN 1-55874-016-3 $7.95

ADDICTIVE RELATIONSHIPS: Reclaiming Your Boundaries
Joy Miller
We have given ourselves away to spouse, lover, children, friends or
parents. By examining where we are, where we want to go and how to get
there, we can reclaim our personal boundaries and the true love of
ourselves.
ISBN 1-55874-003-1 $7.95

RECOVERY FROM CO-DEPENDENCY:
It's Never Too Late To Reclaim Your Childhood
Laurie Weiss, Jonathan B. Weiss
Having been brought up with life-repressing decisions, the adult child
recognizes something isn't working. This book shows how to change
decisions and live differently and fully.
ISBN 0-932194-85-0 $9.95

SHIPPING/HANDLING: All orders shipped UPS unless weight exceeds 200 lbs., special routing is requested, or
delivery territory is outside continental U.S. Orders outside United States shipped either Air Parcel Post or Surface
Parcel Post. Shipping and handling charges apply to all orders shipped whether UPS, Book Rate, Library Rate, Air
or Surface Parcel Post or Common Carrier and will be charged as follows. Orders less than $25.00 in value add
$2.00 minimum. Orders from $25.00 to $50.00 in value (after discount) add $2.50 minimum. Orders greater than
$50.00 in value (after discount) add 6% of value. Orders greater than $25.00 outside United States add 15% of
value. We are not responsible for loss or damage unless material is shipped UPS. Allow 3-5 weeks after receipt of
order for delivery. Prices are subject to change without prior notice.

Enterprise Center, 3201 S.W. 15th Street,
Deerfield Beach, FL 33442-8124
1-800-851-9100

 Health
Communications, Inc.

Other Books By . . .
Health Communications

ADULT CHILDREN OF ALCOHOLICS
Janet Woititz
Over a year on *The New York Times* Best-Seller list, this book is the primer on Adult Children of Alcoholics.
ISBN 0-932194-15-X   **$6.95**

STRUGGLE FOR INTIMACY
Janet Woititz
Another best-seller, this book gives insightful advice on learning to love more fully.
ISBN 0-932194-25-7   **$6.95**

DAILY AFFIRMATIONS: For Adult Children of Alcoholics
Rokelle Lerner
These positive affirmations for every day of the year paint a mental picture of your life as you choose it to be.
ISBN 0-932194-27-3   **$6.95**

CHOICEMAKING: For Co-dependents, Adult Children and Spirituality Seekers — Sharon Wegscheider-Cruse
This useful book defines the problems and solves them in a positive way.
ISBN 0-932194-26-5   **$9.95**

LEARNING TO LOVE YOURSELF: Finding Your Self-Worth
Sharon Wegscheider-Cruse
"Self-worth is a choice, not a birthright," says the author as she shows us how we can choose positive self-esteem.
ISBN 0-932194-39-7   **$7.95**

BRADSHAW ON: THE FAMILY: A Revolutionary Way of Self-Discovery
John Bradshaw
The host of the nationally televised series of the same name shows us how families can be healed and individuals can realize full potential.
ISBN 0-932194-54-0   **$9.95**

HEALING THE CHILD WITHIN:
Discovery and Recovery for Adult Children of Dysfunctional Families
Charles Whitfield
Dr. Whitfield defines, describes and discovers how we can reach our Child Within to heal and nurture our woundedness.
ISBN 0-932194-40-0   **$8.95**

Enterprise Center, 3201 S.W. 15th Street,
Deerfield Beach, FL 33442
1-800-851-9100

Health Communications, Inc.

Daily Affirmation Books from . . .
Health Communications

GENTLE REMINDERS FOR CO-DEPENDENTS: Daily Affirmations
Mitzi Chandler
With insight and humor, Mitzi Chandler takes the co-dependent and the adult child through the year. Gentle Reminders is for those in recovery who seek to enjoy the miracle each day brings.
ISBN 1-55874-020-1 $6.95

TIME FOR JOY: Daily Affirmations
Ruth Fishel
With quotations, thoughts and healing energizing affirmations these daily messages address the fears and imperfections of being human, guiding us through self-acceptance to a tangible peace and the place within where there is *time for joy.*
ISBN 0-932194-82-6 $6.95

CRY HOPE: Positive Affirmations For Healthy Living
Jan Veltman
This book gives positive daily affirmations for seekers and those in recovery. Every day is a new adventure, and change is a challenge.
ISBN 0-932194-74-5 $6.95

SAY YES TO LIFE: Daily Affirmations For Recovery
Father Leo Booth
These meditations take you through the year day by day with Father Leo Booth, looking for answers and sometimes discovering that there are none. Father Leo tells us, "For the recovering compulsive person God is too important to miss — may you find Him now."
IBN 0-932194-46-X $6.95

DAILY AFFIRMATIONS: For Adult Children of Alcoholics
Rokelle Lerner
Affirmations are a way to discover personal awareness, growth and spiritual potential, and self-regard. Reading this book gives us an opportunity to nurture ourselves, learn who we are and what we want to become.
ISBN 0-932194-47-3
(Little Red Book) $6.95
(New Cover Edition) $6.95

Enterprise Center, 3201 S.W. 15th Street,
Deerfield Beach, FL 33442
1-800-851-9100

Health Communications, Inc.

Helpful 12-Step Books from . . .
Health Communications

HEALING A BROKEN HEART:
12 Steps of Recovery for Adult Children
Kathleen W.

This useful 12-Step book is presently the number one resource for all Adult Children support groups.

ISBN 0-932194-65-6   **$7.95**

12 STEPS TO SELF-PARENTING For Adult Children
Philip Oliver-Diaz and Patricia A. O'Gorman

This gentle 12-Step guide takes the reader from pain to healing and self-parenting, from anger to forgiveness, and from fear and despair to recovery.

ISBN 0-932194-68-0   **$7.95**

THE 12-STEP STORY BOOKLETS
Mary M. McKee

Each beautifully illustrated booklet deals with a step, using a story from nature in parable form. The 12 booklets (one for each step) lead us to a better understanding of ourselves and our recovery.

ISBN 1-55874-002-3   **$8.95**

WITH GENTLENESS, HUMOR AND LOVE:
A 12-Step Guide for Adult Children in Recovery
Kathleen W. and Jewell E.

Focusing on adult child issues such as reparenting the inner child, self-esteem, intimacy and feelings, this well-organized workbook teaches techniques and tools for the 12-step recovery programs.

ISBN 0-932194-77-X   **$7.95**

GIFTS FOR PERSONAL GROWTH & RECOVERY
Wayne Kritsberg

A goldmine of positive techniques for recovery (affirmations, journal writing, visualizations, guided meditations, etc.), this book is indispensable for those seeking personal growth.

ISBN 0-932194-60-5   **$6.95**

Enterprise Center, 3201 S.W. 15th Street,
Deerfield Beach, FL 33442
1-800-851-9100

Health
Communications, Inc.